TEEN RIGHTS AND FREEDOMS

| Dress

TEEN RIGHTS AND FREEDOMS

I Dress

Roman Espejo

GREENHAVEN PRESS
A part of Gale, Cengage Learning

GALE
CENGAGE Learning·

Detroit • New York • San Francisco • New Haven, Conn • Waterville, Maine • London

Elizabeth Des Chenes, *Managing Editor*

© 2012 Greenhaven Press, a part of Gale, Cengage Learning

Gale and Greenhaven Press are registered trademarks used herein under license.

For more information, contact:
Greenhaven Press
27500 Drake Rd.
Farmington Hills, MI 48331-3535
Or you can visit our Internet site at gale.cengage.com.

For product information and technology assistance, contact us at:

Gale Customer Support, 1-800-877-4253.
For permission to use material from this text or product, submit all requests online at www.cengage.com/permissions.

Further permissions questions can be emailed to permissionrequest@cengage.com.

Articles in Greenhaven Press anthologies are often edited for length to meet page requirements. In addition, original titles of these works are changed to clearly present the main thesis and to explicitly indicate the author's opinion. Every effort is made to ensure the Greenhaven Press accurately reflects the original intent of the authors. Every effort has been made to trace the owners of copyrighted material.

Cover Image © Darren Greenwood/Design Pics Inc./Alamy.

LIBRARY OF CONGRESS CATALOGING-IN-PUBLICATION DATA

Dress / Roman Espejo, book editor.
    p. cm. -- (Teen rights and freedoms)
    Includes bibliographical references and index.
    ISBN 978-0-7377-5823-8 (hardcover)
1. Freedom of expression--United States. 2. Dress codes--Law and legislation--United States. 3. Students--Civil rights--United States. 4. Students--Legal status, laws, etc.--United States. I. Espejo, Roman, 1977-
    KF4770 .D74
    342.7308'5--dc23

                                            2011043217

Printed in the United States of America
2 3 4 5 6 7 16 15 14 13 12

Contents

1. **School Dress Codes, Free Speech, and the US Courts: An Overview**

   Michael A. Owsley

   A lawyer examines the legal standards established by the Supreme Court that apply to school dress codes and students' freedom of expression through clothing.

2. **Students Have a Right to Free Expression on Clothing When It Does Not Cause Disruption**

   The Supreme Court's Decision

   Abe Fortas

   The Supreme Court maintains that students do not forfeit their First Amendment protections at schools and reserve the right to symbolic speech through dress unless it is disruptive to education or impinges on others' rights.

3. **Disruptive Clothing Is Not Linked to Student Behavior**

   Melinda Swafford, Lee Ann Jolley, and Leigh Southward

   Three professors insist that research finds no significant relationship between disruptive clothing worn by students and behavioral problems at schools.

4. **Schools May Not Prohibit Students from Wearing the Confederate Flag**

   The Circuit Court's Decision

A professor of Latin American studies claims that school dress codes single out minority students, coercing them conform to dominant social norms.

A founder of a libertarian website argues that school uniforms punish the student body for the actions of individuals and do not identify the actual root causes of problems with behavior or academic performance.

Foreword

*"In the truest sense freedom cannot be
bestowed, it must be achieved."*

Franklin D. Roosevelt,
September 16, 1936

The notion of children and teens having rights is a relatively recent development. Early in American history, the head of the household—nearly always the father—exercised complete control over the children in the family. Children were legally considered to be the property of their parents. Over time, this view changed, as society began to acknowledge that children have rights independent of their parents, and that the law should protect young people from exploitation. By the early twentieth century, more and more social reformers focused on the welfare of children, and over the ensuing decades advocates worked to protect them from harm in the workplace, to secure public education for all, and to guarantee fair treatment for youths in the criminal justice system. Throughout the twentieth century, rights for children and teens—and restrictions on those rights—were established by Congress and reinforced by the courts. Today's courts are still defining and clarifying the rights and freedoms of young people, sometimes expanding those rights and sometimes limiting them. Some teen rights are outside the scope of public law and remain in the realm of the family, while still others are determined by school policies.

Each volume in the Teen Rights and Freedoms series focuses on a different right or freedom and offers an anthology of key essays and articles on that right or freedom and the responsibilities that come with it. Material within each volume is drawn from a diverse selection of primary and secondary sources— journals, magazines, newspapers, nonfiction books, organization newsletters, position papers, speeches, and government documents, with a particular emphasis on Supreme Court and lower court decisions. Volumes also include first-person narratives from young people and others involved in teen rights issues, such as parents and educators. The material is selected and arranged to highlight all the major social and legal controversies relating to the right or freedom under discussion. Each selection is preceded by an introduction that provides context and background. In many cases, the essays point to the difference between adult and teen rights, and why this difference exists.

Many of the volumes cover rights guaranteed under the Bill of Rights and how these rights are interpreted and protected in regard to children and teens, including freedom of speech, freedom of the press, due process, and religious rights. The scope of the series also encompasses rights or freedoms, whether real or perceived, relating to the school environment, such as electronic devices, dress, Internet policies, and privacy. Some volumes focus on the home environment, including topics such as parental control and sexuality.

Numerous features are included in each volume of Teen Rights and Freedoms:

- An annotated **table of contents** provides a brief summary of each essay in the volume and highlights court decisions and personal narratives.
- An **introduction** specific to the volume topic gives context for the right or freedom and its impact on daily life.
- A brief **chronology** offers important dates associated with the right or freedom, including landmark court cases.
- **Primary sources**—including personal narratives and court decisions—are among the varied selections in the anthology.
- **Illustrations**—including photographs, charts, graphs, tables, statistics, and maps—are closely tied to the text and chosen to help readers understand key points or concepts.

- An annotated list of **organizations to contact** presents sources of additional information on the topic.
- A **for further reading** section offers a bibliography of books, periodical articles, and Internet sources for further research.
- A comprehensive subject **index** provides access to key people, places, events, and subjects cited in the text.

Each volume of Teen Rights and Freedoms delves deeply into the issues most relevant to the lives of teens: their own rights, freedoms, and responsibilities. With the help of this series, students and other readers can explore from many angles the evolution and current expression of rights both historic and contemporary.

Introduction

Since the 1960s youths seeking to defend their freedom of dress have challenged American schools under the Constitution, as assured by the Free Speech Clause of the First Amendment: "Congress shall make no law . . . abridging the freedom of speech." Like the freedom of expression, however, the freedom of dress is not absolute, particularly for students. This is demonstrated by pivotal cases in the nation's courts, wherein complex case law interpretations and judicial reasoning abound.

In cases involving dress and free speech at schools, the courts defer to *Tinker v. Des Moines Independent Community School District* (1969), the Supreme Court decision that defined the rights and limits of student expression. In 1965 three Iowa students wore black armbands to their schools—armbands that were barred by their principals—in opposition to the Vietnam War and were suspended until the end of their protest. The Court in *Tinker* ruled in favor of the students, arguing that "school officials do not possess absolute authority over their students. Students in school, as well as out of school, are 'persons' under our Constitution." On the other hand, the Court established that school officials have authority over student expression or behaviors that "materially and substantially interfere with the requirements of appropriate discipline in the operation of the school," but such measures must go beyond "a mere desire to avoid the discomfort and unpleasantness that always accompany an unpopular viewpoint." While divisive, the students' armbands did not meet the Court's criteria for disruptive speech.

The lower courts have interpreted the *Tinker* standard in numerous ways, resulting in dissimilar outcomes in suits that involve schools and controversial T-shirts. In *Castorina v. Madison County School Board* (2001), two Kentucky students who wore concert T-shirts bearing the Confederate flag in commemoration of their heritage were suspended in 1997 and sued their school for violating their First Amendment rights. The case was dismissed by a federal district court, but the US Circuit Court of Appeals for the Sixth Circuit reinstated it, arguing that the T-shirts did not cause a material disruption on campus and failed to meet *Tinker*. However, in *Harper v. Poway Unified School District* (2006), the US Circuit Court of Appeals for the Ninth Circuit upheld the ejection of a California student from class after he refused to remove his anti-gay T-shirt in disagreement of the school's observance of homophobia and bullying awareness. The Ninth Circuit decided that the circumstances of the case fulfilled *Tinker* and the T-shirt debased homosexual students and caused substantial interference; the school had already experienced conflicts based on sexual orientation. The Supreme Court, nonetheless, vacated the Ninth Circuit's opinion and remanded it to the district court, from which it was ultimately dismissed.

Other Supreme Court decisions are also applied as standards in cases of student expression and clothing. *Bethel School District v. Fraser* (1986) established that vulgar or offensive speech at functions related to school can be restricted without breaching the Constitution. In this case, the Court reversed a decision by a district court that ruled in favor of the First Amendment rights of a student who was suspended for delivering a sexually suggestive speech. Under *Fraser*, T-shirts of rock band Marilyn Manson were effectively prohibited from an Ohio campus. Additionally *Hazelwood School District v. Kuhlmeier* (1988) determined that student expression in school-endorsed forums has limited First Amendment protections. The Court in *Hazelwood* affirmed that a principal's elimination of stories from a student newspaper was constitutional. In the *Castorina* case, the Sixth Circuit applied the *Hazelwood* standard, maintaining that the students' Confederate flag T-shirts were not school-endorsed speech and thereby fully shielded by the Constitution.

The constitutionality of school dress codes has also been contested, reaching the Sixth Circuit in *Blau v. Fort Thomas Public School District* (2005). A father of a Texas student who was suspended for violating her school's clothing policy filed a suit on the basis that her freedom of speech through dress and his parental rights were infringed. However the Sixth Circuit ruled against them, insisting that the First Amendment does not defend vague expressions of style and individuality. Decades earlier a similar suit, *Karr v. Schmidt* (1972), was brought to the Fifth Circuit. A male high school student in Texas sought equal protection and due process as well as an injunction when the school board prevented him from enrolling for his junior year due to his hair length. "Is there a constitutionally protected right to wear one's hair in a public high school in the length and style that suits the wearer? We hold that no such right is to be found within the plain meaning of the Constitution," stated the Fifth Circuit. "This classification is not based on the 'suspect' criterion of race or wealth," it continued, "which would require application of the 'rigorous' standard of equal protection scrutiny."

Dress is vital to how adolescents explore and express their individuality, and developments in recent years—such as Muslim headscarves and outward experiments in gender identity—continue to spark controversies and reanimate debates. While legal standards for student speech like *Tinker, Fraser,* and *Hazelwood* offer guidance to the lower courts in decisions involving the freedom of dress, a one-size-fits-all approach is not suitable in the balance of individual rights and the authority of schools. *Teen Rights and Freedoms: Dress* investigates these key cases and the issues that impact what young people wear.

Chronology

1969   The Supreme Court issues its opinion in *Tinker v. Des Moines Independent Community School District*, stating that students do not "shed their constitutional rights to freedom of speech or expression at the schoolhouse gate" and may wear clothing with political messages, but that disruptive speech may be regulated by school officials.

1972   In *Karr v. Schmidt* the US Circuit Court of Appeals for the Fifth Circuit rules 8-7 against a male student with long hair, contending that students' choice of hairstyles is not constitutionally protected.

1986   The Supreme Court rules in *Bethel School District v. Fraser* that a school's disciplinary action against a student who gave a sexually suggestive assembly speech did not violate his First Amendment rights.

1987   Cherry Hill Elementary School in Baltimore, Maryland, becomes the first public school recognized for its requirement of uniforms for students.

1988   The Supreme Court affirms in *Hazelwood School District v. Kuhlmeier* that student speech endorsed by schools in any way may be regulated by school officials.

2001

The US Circuit Court of Appeals for the Sixth Circuit decides in *Castorina v. Madison County School Board* that the school suspension of two students for wearing Confederate flags on their T-shirts, in the absence of school disruption, violated their free speech rights.

2004

After an eleven-year-old Muslim girl in Oklahoma was suspended from school for wearing *hijab*, the Muskogee School District and the US Justice Department come to an agreement that makes exceptions for religious clothing in dress codes.

2005

The US Circuit Court of Appeals for the Sixth Circuit rules in *Blau v. Fort Thomas Public School District* that school dress codes are constitutional and student clothing without a particularized message or symbolic meaning is not protected by the First Amendment.

2006

In *Harper v. Poway Unified School District* the US Circuit Court of Appeals for the Ninth Circuit affirms the removal of a student from class, insisting that his anti-gay T-shirt impinged on homosexual students' rights and threatened to cause school disruption.

2007	In *Brandt v. Board of Education of City of Chicago* the US Circuit Court of Appeals for the Seventh Circuit ruled in favor of a school's disciplinary action against students wearing a banned T-shirt in protest of the school's T-shirt contest, claiming that the banned shirts did not become protected speech because they were worn in protest.
2008	A fifteen-year-old gay student who cross-dressed, Lawrence King, was fatally shot by a fourteen-year-old classmate, Brandon McInerney, at E.O. Green Junior High School in Oxnard, California.
2008	The police department of Flint, Michigan, announces an ordinance against sagging pants; punishments include ninety-three days to one year in jail or up to five hundred dollars in fines.
2009	The US Circuit Court of Appeals for the Fifth Circuit in *Paul Palmer v. Waxahachie Independent School District* upholds that schools are permitted to enforce dress codes that restrict student expression on a content-neutral basis.
2010	Twenty-five students attending Oxford High School's prom in Oxford, Alabama, receive dress code violations and must choose between a three-day suspension and paddling as punishment.

> "These three cases have not produced a
> unified doctrine for students' free speech
> rights, but they have carved out three
> separate standards to be used depending
> on the facts of the particular situation."

School Dress Codes, Free Speech, and the US Courts: An Overview

Michael A. Owsley

Michael A. Owsley is a partner at the law firm English Lucas Priest and Owsley in Bowling Green, Kentucky. In the following viewpoint, he surveys the legal standards set by Supreme Court cases involving student speech and how they apply to school dress codes. The author states that the 1967 Tinker case established that clothing with messages cannot be restricted unless it is materially disruptive. The 1986 Fraser case affirmed the lack of constitutional protection for vulgar speech at schools and school-related functions, Owsley explains. And the 1988 Hazelwood case, he adds, determined that school-sponsored student speech can be controlled or censored. Owsley concludes that when a dress code violation is not proven to interfere with the educational process, the school will have difficulty prevailing in court.

It has been over 40 years since John Tinker, Chris Eckhardt, and Mary Beth Tinker were suspended from school when they showed their objections to the hostilities in Vietnam in December 1965 by each wearing a black armband to school in Des Moines, Iowa, but the topic of dress codes and free speech at school is still hot today. In the *Tinker* decision, the Supreme Court found for the students, holding that regulation of student speech is generally permissible only when the speech would "materially and substantially interfere with the requirements of appropriate discipline in the operation of the school." *Tinker* requires a specific and significant fear of disruption, not just some remote apprehension of disturbance. The Court found that students do not "shed their constitutional rights to freedom of speech or expression at the schoolhouse gate."

In 1986 the Supreme Court upheld the suspension of a student for using an elaborate, explicit sexual metaphor in a nominating speech before a student assembly when he had been told that the speech was inappropriate by two teachers. In the *Fraser* decision, the Court determined that the First Amendment does not protect students' use of vulgar and offensive language in public discourse and held that school authorities can punish school-related student speech, which they rationally consider to be "inappropriate and inconsistent with educational objectives."

In 1988 the Supreme Court held that "[E]ducators do not offend the First Amendment by exercising editorial control over the style and content of student speech in school-sponsored expressive activities so long as their actions are reasonably related to legitimate pedagogical concerns." In the *Hazelwood* case, a public high school principal ordered several pages deleted from the school newspaper, which was produced by a journalism class. The articles dealt with students' experiences with pregnancy and the impact of divorce on students at the school. The Supreme Court found that the principal's actions were not unconstitutional and reasoned that the paper was not a public forum because it was produced in a journalism class in which the teacher had final authority over production and publication.

Effects of *Tinker, Fraser,* and *Hazelwood*

These three cases have not produced a unified doctrine for students' free speech rights, but they have carved out three separate standards to be used depending on the facts of the particular situation.

If the expression is passive, symbolic, and/or political, then, pursuant to *Tinker*, school officials must determine its disruptive potential, but must act from more than a simple need to avoid an uncomfortable situation and must be uniform in their application. If school officials are displeased with the "manner" of the speech due to its vulgarity or offensiveness, they may regulate such speech according to *Fraser*. Finally, if the speech or expression is sponsored by the school or in any way bears the school's endorsement, *Hazelwood* permits school officials to determine whether the speech is appropriate.

Are Student Dress Codes Constitutional?

Dress codes have emerged as a means of reducing and preventing violence. These policies are typically aimed at deterring serious offenses by students, such as possession of weapons, drugs, alcohol, and tobacco.

The adoption of a dress code in the Fort Thomas Public School District in Kentucky was challenged in court and the dress code was upheld. The court found that the authority provided under KRS 160.345(2)(c)(1) was reasonable and legitimate and that the dress code adopted by a middle school did not violate a student's First Amendment right to freedom of expression, her substantive due process right to wear the clothes of her choosing, or her parent's substantive due process right to control the dress of his child. The dress code did not interfere with the father's right to direct the education of his daughter and there was no due process violation, as the father had ample knowledge of the dress code proposal and had even attended meetings where it was discussed. The complaint did not allege any religious objection to the code or express the desire to convey a particular message through attire. School districts have the constitutional right to utilize a student dress code. The First Amendment only protects student conduct that conveys a particularized message that can be understood by those who view it.

When Is Student Clothing Considered Speech?

Student clothing is considered speech if it sends a particular message and the message is capable of being understood by others. If clothing is not speech, a school can discipline the student as long as there is a legitimate reason. If clothing is speech, a school can discipline the student only if there is a compelling reason. This continues to be a litigated area involving attempts of various schools to ban certain items of clothing and certain racial symbols. The federal courts continue to define the parameters under the First Amendment.

What Can Be Restricted?

Marilyn Manson T-shirts: A school is allowed to censor speech that is reasonably viewed as promoting illegal drug use. Clothing that is found to be offensive under school dress code policies, such as Marilyn Manson T-shirts, have been successfully restricted under *Fraser*. The court held that the school prohibited the T-shirts because the musical group promotes "disruptive and demoralizing values, which are inconsistent with and counterproductive to education."

Logos: A U.S. District Court held that a Jefferson County school uniform policy is content neutral even if it prohibits logos other

Bans on body piercings in schools have been upheld by courts. © ColorBlind Images/Getty Images.

than that of the school. Items of clothing such as logos, shorts, cargo pants, jeans, jewelry worn outside uniforms, and other items, can be banned by the student dress code policy if the policy is reasonably related to the legitimate educational objectives of avoiding school disruption, fighting, and gang-related issues.

Anti-Nazi Patches: An "anti-Nazi" patch was found to likely cause a substantial disruption of school activities and the removal of the patch did not violate the student's First Amendment rights. This particular high school had a history of violent threats and bullying between two rival cliques.

Clothing Worn As Protest: The Seventh Circuit ruled that a group of students who were disciplined for wearing a banned T-shirt to protest the outcome of the school's official T-shirt contest were not engaged in expression protected by the First

Amendment. Each year the eighth grade students at Beaubien Elementary School choose a class T-shirt from designs submitted by the students. A group of students in the gifted program voted for one particular T-shirt design. When that T-shirt design did not win the contest and the teacher refused to explain her runoff system, the "gifties" (as the students in the gifted program called themselves) wore T-shirts with the losing design and the words "Gifties 2003" instead of wearing the T-shirt that was the winner of the contest, as a form of protest. The vice-principal had previously told the students that if they wore the "Gifties" shirt, they would violate the school's uniform discipline code. The court found that the T-shirts did not become protected expression merely because they were worn in protest. The court also concluded that even if the T-shirt was speech, school officials had the authority to ban the shirts based on the holding in *Hazelwood* that "a school need not tolerate student speech that is inconsistent with its 'basic educational mission.'"

Hair Styles: A Louisiana school policy barring male students from wearing braids was determined to deserve further consideration as possible gender discrimination, but a student's claims of race discrimination and First Amendment violations were found to have no merit. The court relied on *Karr v. Schmidt*, which held that there is no constitutional right "to wear one's hair in a public high school in the length and style that suits the wearer" and rejected the student's claim that his First Amendment rights were violated in denying a hairstyle of choice, particularly favored by African-American males.

Clothing and Jewelry Requirements: The constitutionality of a Nevada high school's mandatory uniform dress code was upheld in a lawsuit that claimed it violated the students' rights to free exercise of religion and free speech. The school adopted a "dress restriction" requiring students to wear khaki pants and red, white or blue shirts with no printed materials. A student was suspended for failing to comply with the restriction when she failed to abide by the policy and wore shirts bearing religious messages. The court held that, for clothing to be considered to be expressive, the wearer must have the "intent to convey a particularized message," and it must be very likely that the message would be understood by observers. The court held that student attire may indeed constitute speech on many levels, and thereby implicate First Amendment rights. Students who sought to wear religious articles were entitled to First Amendment protection but others, who had no intent to convey any particular message, had no such protection.

The Seventh Circuit upheld the student code of conduct and denied a student's request for a preliminary injunction that would have allowed her to wear body-piercing jewelry to her high school. The code of conduct limited pierced jewelry to the ears while the student wore pierced jewelry on her body and she had piercings on her tongue, nasal septum, lip, navel and chest. The court held that a reasonable person would not interpret the body jewelry as conveying any type of message, whether particularized or less specific.

What Cannot Be Restricted?

Political Speech: Some examples of dress that are considered speech are a "Bush Stinks" T-shirt, political buttons, or any item that expresses a particularized message capable of being understood. Student religious speech cannot be curtailed unless the school can show an absolutely compelling reason to do so, and that there are no less restrictive alternatives available. A Vermont school district violated a student's free speech rights when it disciplined the student for wearing a T-shirt critical of President Bush that featured drug and alcohol related images and text.

Views Regarding Abortion: A school district in New York could not ban a T-shirt that proclaimed, "Abortion is Homicide." The court determined that the school district was attempting to regulate the content of the student's political speech. Since there was no evidence of a material or substantial disruption in the school, the message met the *Tinker* standard and could not be banned.

What May Sometimes Be Restricted

Lifestyle Comments: The Ninth Circuit held that the District Court properly denied the student's request for a preliminary injunction when the school officials would not permit the student to wear a T-shirt to high school with the words "Be Ashamed, Our School Embraced What God Has Condemned" on the front and "Homosexuality Is Shameful. Romans 1:27" on the back. The court held that public schools could restrict student speech that intruded upon the rights of other students.

However, the Seventh Circuit held that a student was entitled to a preliminary injunction as he was likely to succeed on the merits of his claim that the school would violate his free speech rights by preventing him from wearing a T-shirt with the slogan "Be Happy, Not Gay."

The Confederate Flag: There is increasing activity on behalf of the Sons of Confederate Veterans to challenge schools that ban the Confederate flag. Schools should not ban the Confederate flag unless there has been a history of racial conflict and permitting the Confederate flag to be displayed would materially and substantially interfere with the requirements of appropriate discipline in the operations of the schools. In some schools, there may be sufficient history of racial animus to justify banning the Confederate flag on clothing. In others there may not. A fact specific inquiry must be conducted to make that determination.

The U.S. Court of Appeals for the Sixth Circuit held that the decisions of two Kentucky students to wear Hank Williams, Jr. T-shirts, in order to commemorate the birthday of Hank Williams, Sr. and to express their southern heritage, constituted free speech under the First Amendment. The T-shirts contained the symbol of the Confederate flag, which the school principal found to be in violation of the dress code. After the students refused to take off or turn the T-shirts inside out, the principal suspended them.

In determining that the students' conduct qualified as speech protected by the First Amendment, the court applied the Supreme Court's standard in *Texas v. Johnson* and determined that the students had intent to convey a particular message and that the message was "easily ascertainable by observers." The court could not determine from the facts whether school officials had selectively applied the dress code to some racially sensitive symbols but not others or whether the school had a history of racial violence necessitating the ban. The case was remanded for trial with instructions that the district court apply *Tinker* in determining whether the students' speech was protected by the First Amendment.

However, in 2007, the U.S. Court of Appeals for the Sixth Circuit ruled that officials at a Tennessee high school did not violate students' free speech rights by prohibiting clothing that depicts the Confederate battle flag. The principal told students wearing clothing with Confederate flags on them that they would be suspended unless they covered up the symbols or removed the shirts. The Blount County Schools' dress code prohibits clothing that "causes disruption to the educational process." The students sued, claiming that their free speech rights were violated; that the school has permitted other controversial expressions, such as foreign flags, Malcolm X symbols, and political slogans; and that no disruption has resulted from the flag. School officials responded by reporting on racial tensions at the school during the 2004–05 and 2005–06 school years that required the stationing of county sheriff's department deputies at the school. Blount County Schools had concluded that wearing the Confederate flag had a significant disruptive effect on the ability of school officials to maintain a proper education environment.

The Sixth Circuit rejected the plaintiffs' contention that the lower court's finding "requires a presumption that the Confederate flag is per se 'racially divisive' and in essence rises to the level of judicially noticed fact." Noting that other courts have taken notice of the inherently racially divisive nature of the Confederate flag, the Sixth Circuit stated that "even if some recognition of the flag's racially divisive nature is implicit in the district court's finding, that finding is not rendered clearly erroneous thereby," and, "even assuming that no students' wearing of that symbol had caused a disruptive incident in the past, the district court nonetheless reasonably could conclude that displays of the Confederate flag would be likely to lead to unrest in the future."

The court also declined to find that the dress code was enforced in a viewpoint specific manner. The court found that the U.S. Supreme Court's decision in *Tinker* does not require that "the banned form of expression itself actually have been the source of past disruptions." Rather, "subsequent appellate court decisions considering school bans on expression have focused on whether the banned conduct would likely trigger disturbances such as those experienced in the past." During the prior school year, the court noted, Blount "had been the scene of racial tension, intimidation and violence to such an extent that law enforcement officials were brought in to maintain order, and the school was defending against lawsuits depicting it as a racially hostile educational environment."

A West Virginia high school faced a situation where the high school student population was 98.6% white and had had only one racial incident early in the 2004–05 school year, which involved the defacing of an African-American student's notebook with racial slurs. In prior years, the school board's dress code did not mention Confederate flags but did disallow dressing or grooming "in a manner that disrupts the educational process or is detrimental to the health, safety or welfare of others."

A new principal began working in the school in the 2004–05 school year and her experience at three other schools included serious incidences of racial violence that involved the use of the Confederate flags. Shortly thereafter, the high school added a ban on "the Rebel flag" to the dress code. The student who was subsequently disciplined wore a shirt depicting the Confederate flag to school almost every day and also had a belt buckle depicting the flag that he wore to school each day. The new principal confronted the student and explained the Confederate flags were banned from school and placed him in detention for violating the ban. The student sued the district, school board and principal for First Amendment violations.

Specific and Significant Fear of Disruption

The court held that schools may prohibit students' speech or conduct that is materially disruptive, involves substantial disorder or invades the rights of others. However, a school must show a specific and significant fear of disruption, not just a remote apprehension of disturbance, in order to suppress student speech.

There was evidence the school did not enforce its ban on prohibited messages related to alcohol and other expressions, such as "Malcolm X" T-shirts. Approximately 75% of the school's students wore flag paraphernalia to school prior to the policy change without complaints or racial incidences.

The court held that school boards could ban racially divisive symbols only where there had been actual racially motivated violence and when a policy was enforced without viewpoint discrimination. The court held it was unnecessary to ban the Confederate flag to maintain school order and discipline and that the policy could not be used to bar lawful, non-violent and non-threatening symbols.

Here the court held that the principal had acted with only a remote apprehension of disturbance, not a specific and significant threat of disruption, and the applicable prohibition in the dress code was invalid. However, the court cautioned that its opinion should not be interpreted as a "safe haven" for those who

The Courts' Inclinations

More recently, the courts have been inclined to uphold reasonable student dress codes as long as the policies allow students to legitimately express themselves on political issues. However, the courts have held that the right to wear fashionable clothing is not, in itself, a fundamental right protected by the Constitution. In addition, the courts give wide latitude to policy makers to develop dress codes that regulate obscene or lewd speech and gang-related clothing. The courts have been inclined to support school uniform policies, allowing local-level policy makers to determine what is best for their schools. However, because school uniform policies tend to be viewed as directive, an "opt out" policy is a common means of avoiding potential litigation.

John P. Renaud and Asterie Baker Provenzo,
Encyclopedia of the Social and Cultural Foundations of Education, Volume 2. *Thousand Oaks, CA: SAGE, 2009.*

would use the flag for disruption or intimidation. Should that occur, the very ban that it struck down might then be appropriate.

If a school cannot show that violations of the dress code have had a disruptive effect on the educational process, it will be difficult to prevail if a student challenges the dress code. The standards set in *Tinker, Hazelwood,* and *Fraser* are still good today and should be followed when addressing school dress codes. School officials should carefully review the factual situation they face to determine if the accepted legal standards have been violated and that those standards are being uniformly applied before banning items of clothing.

> "The prohibition of the silent, passive 'witness of the armbands,' as one of the children called it, is no less offensive to the Constitution's guarantees."

Students Have a Right to Free Expression on Clothing When It Does Not Cause Disruption

The Supreme Court's Decision

Abe Fortas

In 1965 three students in Des Moines, Iowa, were suspended from school for wearing black armbands on campus in protest of the Vietnam War. The case, Tinker v. Des Moines Independent Community School District, *reached the Supreme Court, which overturned a lower court's decision to uphold the school's actions. In the following viewpoint, excerpted from the Supreme Court's opinion, Justice Abe Fortas asserts that the students' choice to wear the armbands was protected by the First Amendment, as it did not cause material disruption or impinge on others' rights. He declares that the suspension resulted from the school district's desire to avoid the controversy of an unpopular opinion, denying the openness of ideas that serves as the foundation of American independence. Fortas served on the Supreme Court from 1965 to 1969.*

The District Court recognized that the wearing of an armband for the purpose of expressing certain views is the type of symbolic act that is within the Free Speech Clause of the First Amendment. As we shall discuss, the wearing of armbands in the circumstances of this case was entirely divorced from actually or potentially disruptive conduct by those participating in it. It was closely akin to "pure speech" which, we have repeatedly held, is entitled to comprehensive protection under the First Amendment. First Amendment rights, applied in light of the special characteristics of the school environment, are available to teachers and students. It can hardly be argued that either students or teachers shed their constitutional rights to freedom of speech or expression at the schoolhouse gate. This has been the unmistakable holding of this Court for almost 50 years. In *Meyer v. Nebraska* (1923) and *Bartels v. Iowa* (1923), this Court, in opinions by Mr. Justice McReynolds, held that the Due Process Clause of the Fourteenth Amendment prevents States from forbidding the teaching of a foreign language to young students. Statutes to this effect, the Court held, unconstitutionally interfere with the liberty of teacher, student, and parent.

In *West Virginia v. Barnette*, this Court held that under the First Amendment, the student in public school may not be compelled to salute the flag. Speaking through Mr. Justice Jackson, the Court said:

> The Fourteenth Amendment, as now applied to the States, protects the citizen against the State itself and all of its creatures—Boards of Education not excepted. These have, of course, important, delicate, and highly discretionary functions, but none that they may not perform within the limits of the Bill of Rights. That they are educating the young for citizenship is reason for scrupulous protection of Constitutional freedoms of the individual, if we are not to strangle the free mind at

William F. Hornsby was suspended in 1965 for wearing a black armband in mourning for Vietnam War dead. In Tinker v. Des Moines School District *the Supreme Court ruled in 1969 that wearing a black armband in class to protest the Vietnam War is protected by the First Amendment.* © AP Images.

its source and teach youth to discount important principles of our government as mere platitudes.

On the other hand, the Court has repeatedly emphasized the need for affirming the comprehensive authority of the States and of school officials, consistent with fundamental constitutional safeguards, to prescribe and control conduct in the schools. Our problem lies in the area where students in the exercise of First Amendment rights collide with the rules of the school authorities.

The problem posed by the present case does not relate to regulation of the length of skirts or the type of clothing, to hair style, or deportment. It does not concern aggressive, disruptive action or even group demonstrations. Our problem involves direct, primary First Amendment rights akin to "pure speech." The school officials banned and sought to punish petitioners for a silent, passive expression of opinion, unaccompanied by any disorder or disturbance on the part of petitioners. There is here no evidence whatever of petitioners' interference, actual or nascent, with the schools' work or of collision with the rights of other students to be secure and to be let alone. Accordingly, this case does not concern speech or action that intrudes upon the work of the schools or the rights of other students.

Only a few of the 18,000 students in the school system wore the black armbands. Only five students were suspended for wearing them. There is no indication that the work of the schools or any class was disrupted. Outside the classrooms, a few students made hostile remarks to the children wearing armbands, but there were no threats or acts of violence on school premises.

The District Court concluded that the action of the school authorities was reasonable because it was based upon their fear of a disturbance from the wearing of the armbands. But, in our system, undifferentiated fear or apprehension of disturbance is not enough to overcome the right to freedom of expression. Any departure from absolute regimentation may cause trouble. Any variation from the majority's opinion may inspire fear. Any word spoken, in class, in the lunchroom, or on the campus, that deviates from the views of another person may start an argument or cause a disturbance. But our Constitution says we must take this risk, and our history says that it is this sort of hazardous freedom—this kind of openness—that is the basis of our national strength and of the independence and vigor of Americans who grow up and live in this relatively permissive, often disputatious, society.

Avoiding the Controversy

In order for the State in the person of school officials to justify prohibition of a particular expression of opinion, it must be able to show that its action was caused by something more than a mere desire to avoid the discomfort and unpleasantness that always accompany an unpopular viewpoint. Certainly where there is no finding and no showing that engaging in the forbidden conduct would "materially and substantially interfere with the requirements of appropriate discipline in the operation of the school," the prohibition cannot be sustained.

In the present case, the District Court made no such finding, and our independent examination of the record fails to yield evidence that the school authorities had reason to anticipate that the wearing of the armbands would substantially interfere with the work of the school or impinge upon the rights of other students. Even an official memorandum prepared after the suspension that listed the reasons for the ban on wearing the armbands made no reference to the anticipation of such disruption.

On the contrary, the action of the school authorities appears to have been based upon an urgent wish to avoid the controversy, which might result from the expression, even by the silent symbol of armbands, of opposition to this Nation's part in the conflagration in Vietnam. It is revealing, in this respect, that the meeting at which the school principals decided to issue the contested regulation was called in response to a student's statement to the journalism teacher in one of the schools that he wanted to write an article on Vietnam and have it published in the school paper. (The student was dissuaded.)

It is also relevant that the school authorities did not purport to prohibit the wearing of all symbols of political or controversial significance. The record shows that students in some of the schools wore buttons relating to national political campaigns, and some even wore the Iron Cross, traditionally a symbol of Nazism. The order prohibiting the wearing of armbands did not extend to these. Instead, a particular symbol—black armbands worn to exhibit opposition to this Nation's involvement in Vietnam—was singled out for prohibition. Clearly, the prohibition of expression of one particular opinion, at least without evidence that it is necessary to avoid material and substantial interference with schoolwork or discipline, is not constitutionally permissible.

Students Have Fundamental Rights

In our system, state-operated schools may not be enclaves of totalitarianism. School officials do not possess absolute authority over their students. Students in school as well as out of school are "persons" under our Constitution. They are possessed of fundamental rights, which the State must respect, just as they themselves must respect their obligations to the State. In our system, students may not be regarded as closed-circuit recipients of only that which the State chooses to communicate. They may not be confined to the expression of those sentiments that are officially approved. In the absence of a specific showing of constitutionally valid reasons to regulate their speech, students are entitled to freedom of expression of their views. As Judge Gewin, speaking for the Fifth Circuit, said, school officials cannot suppress "expressions of feelings with which they do not wish to contend."

In *Meyer v. Nebraska*, Mr. Justice McReynolds expressed this Nation's repudiation of the principle that a State might so conduct its schools as to "foster a homogeneous people." He said:

> In order to submerge the individual and develop ideal citizens, Sparta assembled the males at seven into barracks and entrusted their subsequent education and training to official guardians. Although such measures have been deliberately approved by men of great genius, their ideas touching the relation between individual and State were wholly different from those upon which our institutions rest; and it hardly will be affirmed that any legislature could impose such restrictions upon the people of a State without doing violence to both letter and spirit of the Constitution.

This principle has been repeated by this Court on numerous occasions during the intervening years. In *Keyishian v. Board of Regents*, Mr. Justice Brennan, speaking for the Court, said:

> "The vigilant protection of constitutional freedoms is nowhere more vital than in the community of American schools" (*Shelton v. Tucker*). The classroom is peculiarly the "marketplace of ideas." The Nation's future depends upon leaders trained through wide exposure to that robust exchange of ideas which discovers truth "out of a multitude of tongues, [rather] than through any kind of authoritative selection."

The principle of these cases is not confined to the supervised and ordained discussion, which takes place in the classroom. The principal use to which the schools are dedicated is to accommodate students during prescribed hours for the purpose of certain types of activities. Among those activities is personal intercommunication among the students. This is not only an inevitable part of the process of attending school; it is also an important part of the educational process. A student's rights, therefore, do not embrace merely the classroom hours. When he is in the cafeteria, or on the playing field, or on the campus during the authorized hours, he may express his opinions, even on controversial subjects like the conflict in Vietnam, if he does so without "materially and substantially interfer[ing] with the requirements of appropriate discipline in the operation of the school" and without colliding with the rights of others. But conduct by the student, in class or out of it, which for any reason—whether it stems from time, place, or type of behavior—materially disrupts class work or involves substantial disorder or invasion of the rights of others is, of course, not immunized by the constitutional guarantee of freedom of speech.

The Students Were Denied Their Form of Expression

Under our Constitution, free speech is not a right that is given only to be so circumscribed that it exists in principle but not

The Dissenting Opinion of Justice Hugo Black

One does not need to be a prophet or the son of a prophet to know that after the Court's holding today some students in Iowa schools and indeed in all schools will be ready, able, and willing to defy their teachers on practically all orders. This is the more unfortunate for the schools since groups of students all over the land are already running loose, conducting break-ins, sit-ins, lie-ins, and smash-ins. Many of these student groups, as is all too familiar to all who read the newspapers and watch the television news programs, have already engaged in rioting, property seizures, and destruction. They have picketed schools to force students not to cross their picket lines and have too often violently attacked earnest but frightened students who wanted an education that the pickets did not want them to get. Students engaged in such activities are apparently confident that they know far more about how to operate public school systems than do their parents, teachers, and elected school officials.

Hugo Black, Tinker v. Des Moines Independent Community School District, *US Supreme Court, February 24, 1969.*

in fact. Freedom of expression would not truly exist if the right could be exercised only in an area that a benevolent government has provided as a safe haven for crackpots. The Constitution says that Congress (and the States) may not abridge the right to free speech. This provision means what it says. We properly read it to permit reasonable regulation of speech-connected activities in carefully restricted circumstances. But we do not confine the permissible exercise of First Amendment rights to a telephone booth or the four corners of a pamphlet, or to supervised and ordained discussion in a school classroom.

If a regulation were adopted by school officials forbidding discussion of the Vietnam conflict, or the expression by any student of opposition to it anywhere on school property except as part of a prescribed classroom exercise, it would be obvious that the regulation would violate the constitutional rights of students, at least if it could not be justified by a showing that the students' activities would materially and substantially disrupt the work and discipline of the school. In the circumstances of the present case, the prohibition of the silent, passive "witness of the armbands," as one of the children called it, is no less offensive to the Constitution's guarantees.

As we have discussed, the record does not demonstrate any facts which might reasonably have led school authorities to forecast substantial disruption of or material interference with school activities, and no disturbances or disorders on the school premises in fact occurred. These petitioners merely went about their ordained rounds in school. Their deviation consisted only in wearing on their sleeve a band of black cloth, not more than two inches wide. They wore it to exhibit their disapproval of the Vietnam hostilities and their advocacy of a truce, to make their views known, and, by their example, to influence others to adopt them. They neither interrupted school activities nor sought to intrude in the school affairs or the lives of others. They caused discussion outside of the classrooms, but no interference with work and no disorder. In the circumstances, our Constitution does not permit officials of the State to deny their form of expression.

> *"There is not a significant relationship between the level of offensiveness in attire and a student's behavioral problems at school."*

Disruptive Clothing Is Not Linked to Student Behavior

Melinda Swafford, Lee Ann Jolley, and Leigh Southward

In the following viewpoint, Melinda Swafford, Lee Ann Jolley, and Leigh Southward question the relationship between offensive clothing and risky behaviors. Swafford, Jolley, and Southward acknowledge that what adolescents wear may intentionally or unintentionally reveal information about their personalities, but their research indicates that it has little association with school conduct. Moreover, clothing choices are important in the transition to adulthood, the authors contend, as adolescents consider dress a symbol of identification, self-expression, and social norms. Swafford is an associate professor in family and consumer science, and Jolley is an assistant professor at Tennessee Technological University School of Human Ecology. Southward is an associate professor of apparel studies at the University of Arkansas School of Human Sciences.

School systems across the United States are faced with numerous concerns regarding student dress. Schools often address these concerns by enforcing dress codes, which are sometimes referred to as Appropriate School Attire (ASA), or by mandating school uniforms. The basis behind a school system implementing dress codes or school uniforms ranges from modesty concerns, to health and safety issues, to attempts to ensure that the school's classroom environment is conducive to learning. The issues surrounding a school system's decision to mandate student dress are controversial and, in our view, worthy of careful consideration of adolescent developmental issues. Additionally, we propose that a review of research studies that have attempted to either validate the importance of mandating school dress or discredit their importance is helpful to school systems faced with making such decisions.

Understanding the Mindset of Teens

The teen years are often depicted as being full of conflict, turmoil, alienation, recklessness, risky behaviors and challenges. Conflicts and challenges often surface over issues of dress between parents, school administrators and students. Adolescents may view these conflicts and challenges as a violation of individual rights.

Clothing choices are especially important for adolescents as they interact and make the transition to adulthood. Adolescents view dress as a symbol of identification, self-expression, as well as a regulator of expected behavior. According to [authors D.] Papalia, [S.] Olds, and [R.] Feldman, [psychologist Erik] Erikson identified the chief developmental task of adolescence as the confrontation of the crisis of identity versus identity confusion or identity versus role confusion.

Photo on previous page: Some argue that a student's clothing choices are simply a form of expression and have little correlation to school conduct or performance. © Ricky John Molloy/ Getty Images.

In order to mark progress toward the resolution of this crisis in development, an adolescent seeks to develop a sense of self, determine goals, values and beliefs, and explore what role he or she will play in life. This exploration of life possibilities leads to changes in self-concept and provides the basis for the development of a personal identity. Since peers are an important influence, and forming peer relationships is a major developmental task of adolescence, they tend to conform to the most obvious aspect of peer culture—dress. [Researchers J.] Workman, [N.] Auseneau, and [C.] Ewell suggest that the developmental task of adolescence may be resolved or hindered by clothing choices, as these choices are a reflection of individual expression and are important in peer integration and acceptance.

"Adolescents can use dress (e.g., message T-shirts) to condone attitudes, behaviors, beliefs, values, and group affiliations that simultaneously communicate their identity, autonomy, peer group integration, sociopolitical awareness, individuality, and self-perception," [said] Workman, Auseneau, and Ewell.

Therefore, adolescents' clothing choices may intentionally or unintentionally reveal information about their personalities, backgrounds, interests and contribute to the establishment of a reputation. Workman, Auseneau, and Ewell's study suggests empirical evidence to justify a school system's decision to enforce a school dress code or require school uniforms.

Linking Attire to Behavior

Proponents of school dress codes and school uniforms often attempt to link adolescents' clothing choices to student behaviors. Since adolescents communicate values, self-expression and validate themselves through clothing, it is reasonable to assume that values can be related to behavior. An adolescent's clothing choices are often a reflection of his or her abilities, personal qualities or performance. [Researcher N.] Joseph, as cited [by researchers D.] Brunsma and [K.A.] Rocquemore, asserted that clothing choices can be a sign that conveys a person's values, beliefs and emotions.

Thus, "If the clothing that adolescents wear can be considered a sign, then one can perceive their clothes as an expression of personal identity," [said] Brunsma and Rocquemore. This assertion is validated by [researchers J.E.] Arnold and Workman, whose study [stated] that "students who owned offensive T-shirts were more likely to engage in violent behavior, experience consequences of problem behavior, engage in substance abuse, and have a negative attitude toward school."

Opponents of adopting school dress codes or school uniforms often focus on the legal issues and effectiveness surrounding such policies. Brunsma and Rockquemore examined the data from two large databases—"The 1998 National Educational Longitudinal Study" and the 1998 "Early Childhood Longitudinal Study"—to empirically test the relationship between adolescents' attire, specifically school uniforms, and behavior. Their findings indicate that student uniforms have no direct effect on substance abuse, behavioral problems, school safety, school attendance, or academic achievement.

Family and Consumer Sciences Educators Conduct Survey

As family and consumer sciences teachers, we became curious about the conflicting data regarding adolescent clothing and behaviors and set out to determine if we could find a correlation between what family and consumer sciences students find offensive in clothing choices, and their attendance and behavior in school. Sixty-six students from two rural high schools from a southeastern state were surveyed in a family and consumer sciences class by viewing photographs of T-shirts with various logos, slogans and pictures. (Each student was given a letter of consent that had to be signed by a parent or guardian and returned to the school in order to participate.)

Respondents answered questions regarding level of offensiveness and whether or not they would wear the T-shirt in the photograph. They rated the level of offensiveness using a Likert

Uniforms Do Not Distinguish or Impact Behavior

To state the results . . . in a nutshell, we found that uniform policies did not distinguish between students who had attendance problems, behavioral problems, or substance use problems and those who did not. Furthermore, uniforms failed, in our empirical analyses, to increase academic preparedness, pro-school attitudes, or a peer structure that supported academics. Finally, to our surprise, we found a small, weak, yet statistically significant negative effect of uniform policies on academic achievement. In the end, this was what is typically referred to as a piece of "nonfindings" in scientific discourse; yet in this case the overwhelming pattern of *non*-effectiveness of school uniforms (one way or the other) was of general interest to educators, scholars, and policymakers alike.

David L. Brunsma, The School Uniform Movement and What It Tells Us About American Education. *Lanham, MD: Scarecrow Education, 2004.*

Scale of 1-5. Demographics and information pertaining to the number of times they violated the school dress code or were in in-school suspension or out-of-school suspension were also gathered. Data were analyzed through logistic regression (multiple regression) and ANOVA [analysis of variance] to determine if there was a relationship between their perceptions of offensive T-shirts and their behavior.

Ninety percent of the respondents were female. Twenty-two percent were high school freshman, 41 percent were sophomores, 20 percent juniors, and 16 percent were seniors. Only 23 percent indicated that they had violated the school dress code, with 7.4 percent for inappropriate size violation and 4.4 percent for vulgar attire violation. In addition, 22 percent had indicated they had been in in-school suspension. Only three percent had been in out-of-school suspension. However, 63.2 percent of the students had been absent from school three times or fewer.

The photograph of the T-shirt with the slogan "I pee on toilet seats" had a mean rating of 3.8, which was the highest mean for level of offensiveness, and a 22.1 percent very offensive rating. The T-shirts with the slogans "Got Jesus?" and "You are my beloved son, in whom I am well pleased, Luke 3:22," received the lowest mean of 1.0 on level of offensiveness, 86.8 percent and 83.8 percent, respectively. The majority of the respondents indicated they would wear only a few of the T-shirts to school, with friends, or with family.

The results of this small study indicated there was not a significant relationship between level of offensiveness and behavioral problems at school. The students who reported violating the school dress code or being in a type of school suspension were no more likely to find a certain T-shirt offensive, and they also indicated they were no more likely to wear these T-shirts than those students who responded with no violation of school policies and no type of school suspensions. There was no correlation between school attendance and perception of offensiveness. These results support the research by Brunsma and Rockquemore that adolescent dress does not affect school behaviors. Thus, our data from this study does not lend our support for arguments in favor of school dress codes or school uniforms.

Implications and Court Rulings

What implications, then, does our research study have regarding the debate to require school dress codes or school uniforms? It may depend on the school system's reason for the policy. It is our view that there is not a significant relationship between the level of offensiveness in attire and a student's behavioral problems at school, and the adoption of a dress code policy will not significantly impact school attendance or behavior.

With regard to dress code policies, it is important to note that many court systems attempt to make a distinction between dress codes that govern freedom of expression and those that regulate message content. [Researcher] Weisenberger suggests that a balance test is often used to determine if a dress code appears to be unconstitutional. The balance test weighs several factors, including students' rights, the rights of others, and the rights of educators.

Many school systems advocate that dress codes are less restrictive than school uniform policies. For example, a school system may require students to wear solid colors and ban images and/ or logos on clothing as did a school district in Napa, California. There a student was reprimanded and sent to detention because she wore socks adorned with the Disney images of Winnie-the-Pooh's friend Tigger. However, the student's family sued the school district for violation of the right of freedom of speech. The school district rescinded its decision of a strict dress code to a more lax policy allowing images and fabrics other than solid colors. The school district admitted that banning images on clothing may raise concerns about the restriction of religious and political speech.

In two other important cases, overturned by the United States Supreme Court in 2007, students were suspended from school for violating school dress codes. One Vermont student wore a T-shirt depicting former President George W. Bush surrounded by drug and alcohol images. The Supreme Court stood by a lower court's decision by ruling that the student was protected by free political expression. A student in a San Diego high school was suspended for wearing an anti-gay T-shirt. Again, the Supreme Court ruled against the school system and upheld the student's right to free speech. In both of these situations, the Supreme Court ruled against the school system and in favor of the right to free speech. So, having a school dress code may not even be enforceable by the school district.

Moving Forward

Since T-shirts are common dress for many adolescents, it is our hope that the results of our small but telling research study will help explain what high school students view as offensive as well as how perceptions of offensiveness might affect dress and behavior. This information can be used to guide school administrators as they set dress codes and make decisions relating to school uniforms, and help them gain an understanding of the impact of dress on adolescent identification. In addition, careful consideration should be given to freedom of religious and political expression and to individual rights to the freedom of speech as guaranteed by the United States Constitution. Due to the homogeneity of the sample and response, the authors acknowledge its limitations in regard to sample size and recommend replication with a larger, more diverse sample in order for the results to be generalized to a larger population.

| "Their decision to wear the Hank
Williams T-shirts constitutes speech
falling within the First Amendment."

Schools May Not Prohibit Students from Wearing the Confederate Flag

The Circuit Court's Decision

Gilbert S. Merritt Jr.

In 1997 two students in Madison County, Kentucky, were suspended from school for wearing concert T-shirts of country singer Hank Williams Jr. that bore images of the Confederate flag. In the following opinion excerpted from the US Court of Appeals for the Sixth Circuit's opinion in Castorina v. Madison County School Board, *Justice Gilbert S. Merritt Jr. argues that the federal court ruling upholding the students' suspension violated the First Amendment, and* Fraser *and* Hazelwood—two legal standards regulating student expression—were inapplicable. Merritt insists that the T-shirts were constitutionally protected because they qualified as speech and were not school-sponsored. Additionally he states that other racially sensitive symbols were not banned at the* *school and the Confederate flag worn by the students did not cause a material disruption. Merritt was appointed to the Sixth Circuit in 1977 and became a senior judge in 2001.*

In the fall of 1997, when all of the events in question took place, Timothy Castorina and Tiffany Dargavell were students at Madison Central High School, located in Madison County, Kentucky. Castorina was a junior and Dargavell a freshman. At the time, Castorina and Dargavell were dating. Neither had previously experienced any significant disciplinary problems.

On the morning of September 17, both plaintiffs arrived at school wearing matching Hank Williams, Jr. concert T-shirts given to them by Dargavell's father. Country music star Hank Williams, Jr. was pictured on the front of the T-shirts and two Confederate flags were displayed on the back, along with the phrase "Southern Thunder." The plaintiffs said that they were wearing the T-shirts in commemoration of Hank Williams, Sr.'s birthday and to express their southern heritage. When the two students went to the principal's office to change Dargavell's class schedule, the principal, William Fultz, informed them that the Confederate flag emblem violated the school's dress code. He gave the students the choice of either turning the shirts inside out for the rest of the day or returning home to change. Fultz based this instruction on his interpretation of the school's dress code, which prohibits students from wearing any clothing or emblem "that is obscene, sexually suggestive, disrespectful, or which contains slogans, words or in any way depicts alcohol, drugs, tobacco or any illegal, immoral, or racist implication." The dress code specified that if the violation could not be corrected at school, then the principal had the authority to send the offender home to change and to assign appropriate punishment. When Castorina and Dargavell refused to comply with his directives, Fultz called their parents.

He explained to the parents that the clothing was a violation of the dress code, but that if the parents convinced the students

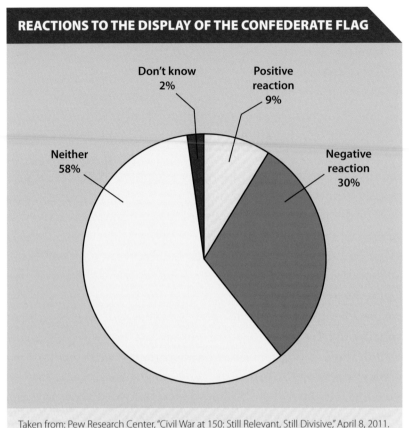

REACTIONS TO THE DISPLAY OF THE CONFEDERATE FLAG

Don't know
2%

Positive
reaction
9%

Neither
58%

Negative
reaction
30%

Taken from: Pew Research Center, "Civil War at 150: Still Relevant, Still Divisive," April 8, 2011.

to go home and change there would be no disciplinary action. If the students refused to change, they would be suspended for three days. The parents strongly supported their children's decision, and Fultz suspended each student. At the end of the three days, Castorina and Dargavell returned to school wearing the same shirts. Fultz again explained that the flag was offensive to other students and a violation of the dress code. When the parents reiterated their support for the students' desire to wear the T-shirts, Fultz suspended them for a second three-day period. Castorina and Dargavell never returned to Madison Central and were subsequently given home-schooling by their parents.

In ruling on the students' suit challenging their suspensions, the district court found that wearing the T-shirts did not qualify as "speech" and that even if it were "speech," the plaintiffs failed to show a First Amendment violation. In addition, the court rejected the plaintiffs' contention that the school dress code was vague and overbroad. The Court then dismissed all supplemental state claims without prejudice.

This case raises two main questions: (1) does wearing the Confederate flag T-shirts qualify as the type of speech covered by the First Amendment, and (2) if so, is that speech protected given the special rules governing schools' authority to regulate student speech? The district court's answer to the first question—that wearing the Hank Williams, Jr. T-shirts did not qualify as "speech"—was incorrect. The plaintiffs wore the shirts to express a certain viewpoint and that viewpoint was easily ascertainable by an observer. On the second question, viewing all of the facts in the light most favorable to the plaintiffs, it appears that the school board enforced the dress code in an uneven and viewpoint-specific manner, thereby violating core values of the First Amendment. In addition, the school has not shown that the plaintiffs' conduct creates a likelihood of violence or other disruption that warrants this kind of regulation.

The Plaintiffs' Conduct Was Speech Governed by the First Amendment

In *Texas v. Johnson* (1989) (the flag-burning case), the Supreme Court laid out the standard for what conduct constitutes expression protected by the First Amendment. This inquiry focused on "whether [a]n intent to convey a particularized message was present and [whether] the likelihood was great that the message would be understood by those who viewed it." In the instant case, the district court concluded that the plaintiffs intended to commemorate Hank Williams, Sr.'s birthday. The court found that this was a particularized message, but that this message was unascertainable based on the plaintiffs' decision to wear a Hank

Williams, Jr. T-shirt. The court characterized the wearing of these T-shirts as a "mere display" of a confederate flag and ruled that this did not result in a finding of protected speech. Both plaintiffs, however, testified that they intended to convey pride in their southern heritage in addition to any message associated with Hank Williams, Sr.

The school board does not dispute the plaintiffs' claim that they also intended to affirm their southern backgrounds. The T-shirts prominently displayed two Confederate flags and the phrase "Southern Thunder." In addition, both Hank Williams, Sr. and Hank Williams, Jr. are singers whose songs have strong appeal in the South. We therefore conclude that the plaintiffs intended to express more than a mere appreciation for the life and music of either performer. Further, their decision to return to school at the end of the first suspension still wearing the T-shirts demonstrates that the students fully appreciated the message that school administrators understood the T-shirts to convey. Because the plaintiffs' intended expression was both a commemoration of Hank Williams, Sr.'s birthday as well as a statement affirming the plaintiffs' shared southern heritage, their decision to wear the Hank Williams T-shirts constitutes speech falling within the First Amendment.

The School Board's Authority to Regulate the Plaintiffs' Speech

This case is governed by the Supreme Court's landmark decision concerning student speech, *Tinker v. Des Moines Independent School District* (1969). While *Tinker* has been narrowed by two more recent cases, *Bethel School District No. 403 v. Fraser* (1986), and *Hazelwood School District v. Kuhlmeier* (1988), neither of these decisions altered *Tinker*'s core principles concerning the circumstances under which public schools may regulate student speech. In *Tinker*, the Supreme Court struck down the school district's ban on the wearing of black armbands to protest the Vietnam War. Central to the decision was the fact that the school district did not ban other clothing that expressed controversial views, including Iron Crosses, which were often understood as symbols of Hitler and the Nazis. This aspect of the decision is consistent with a number of later Supreme Court decisions signaling that viewpoint-specific speech restrictions are an egregious violation of the First Amendment.

In contrast, *Fraser* concerned a school's decision to discipline a student after he used "offensively lewd and indecent speech" during a speech nominating a classmate for a position in the student assembly. The Court found that this was not protected speech and that the school had an interest in teaching students the boundaries of socially appropriate behavior that provided some room for a school to regulate speech, which would otherwise be protected. In *Hazelwood*, the Court upheld the school's decision to censor certain articles in the school newspaper. The Court found that the school newspaper was not a public forum and that school officials are entitled to exercise greater control over "school-sponsored" speech such as a school newspaper. Beyond the three "school-speech" Supreme Court cases and the well-developed line of Supreme Court decisions prohibiting viewpoint discrimination, two Court of Appeals decisions, *Melton v. Young* (6th Cir. 1972), and *West v. Derby Unified School District No. 260*, (10th Cir. 2000), are relevant in that they uphold a public school's authority to ban Confederate flags in somewhat different factual circumstances.

More Analogous to *Tinker*

The facts, when viewed in the light most favorable to the plaintiffs, distinguish the Madison County ban on Confederate flags from the bans upheld in all four of these cases. First, the plaintiffs testified that other members of the student body wore clothing venerating Malcolm X and were not disciplined. Second, the plaintiffs were wearing the disputed clothing in a manner that did not disrupt school activity or cause unrest during the school day. Third, Castorina and Dargavell were clearly making a personal statement in deciding to wear the Hank Williams, Jr. T-shirts; in other words, there is no way that their speech could be considered to be "school-sponsored," nor did the students use any school resources to express their views.

Taking these facts into consideration, the Madison County case is more analogous to *Tinker* than to either *Fraser* or *Hazelwood*. In *Tinker*, the Des Moines school board had adopted a policy specifically banning the wearing of black armbands. The policy stated that any students found in violation would be asked to remove the offending article; if the student refused, suspension would follow until the student returned without the armband. The plaintiffs intentionally violated the policy and were sent home. Following their legal challenge to the suspension, the Supreme Court struck down the school policy as unconstitutional. As a preliminary matter, the Court formally recognized the fact that students do not "shed their constitutional rights to freedom of speech or expression at the schoolhouse gate." Though schools have the authority to set regulations pertaining to the length of skirts or hair, the Court held that there was no basis for a policy that punished "silent, passive expression of opinion, unaccompanied by any disorder or disturbance on the part of petitioners." The Court drew special attention to the fact that the plaintiffs' actions did not cause any interference "with schools' work or collision with the rights of other students to be secure and to be let alone."

In the lower court proceedings, the district court had based its decision upholding the school board's actions on the fear of disturbance, but the Supreme Court rejected this argument because "undifferentiated fear or apprehension of disturbance is not enough to overcome the right to freedom of expression." In addition, the Supreme Court was clearly influenced by the fact that the school board adopted a policy that only banned black armbands, and not other potentially disruptive symbols. For example, the Court specifically noted that the school board banned black armbands while allowing students to wear the Iron Cross,

A US Circuit Court of Appeals ruled in 2001 that wearing the Confederate flag in school is a protected form of free speech. © AP Images/Duncan Mansfield.

a symbol that obviously invoked images of Nazi Germany. In the instant case, Dargavell and Castorina claim that students in Madison County wore clothing bearing the "X" symbol associated with Malcolm X and the Black Muslim movement. The school's refusal to bar the wearing of this apparel along with the Confederate flag gives the appearance of a targeted ban, something that the Supreme Court has routinely struck down as a violation of the First Amendment. The Court has held that this type of ban is a "more blatant" violation of the First Amendment because "government regulation may not regulate speech based on its substantive content or the message it conveys."

Viewing the facts in the light most favorable to the students, the school has banned only certain racial viewpoints without any showing of disruption. As a result, without any formal factual findings to guide us, we see no obvious differences between the *Tinker* and Madison County situations other than the fact that the Des Moines School Board adopted a formal policy banning black armbands before the students ever wore them, whereas the Madison County School Board banned Confederate flags in a more "ad hoc" manner. This means that in *Tinker* there was a formally targeted ban from the very beginning, whereas the Madison County dress code is a facially neutral policy that is enforced, according to the students, in a content-specific manner. If the students' claim is true, only certain ideological positions are barred from expression on school property. Based on the Supreme Court rulings in *Tinker*, *Mosley* and *Rosenberger*, the school board cannot single out Confederate flags for special treatment while allowing other controversial racial and political symbols to be displayed.

Fraser and *Hazelwood* Standards Are Inapplicable

The more recent Supreme Court decisions discussing schools' authority to regulate student speech are not applicable to this situation. Both *Fraser* and *Hazelwood*—the two cases often cited for public schools' power to regulate their students' speech—contain important factual differences that distinguish them from the instant controversy. *Fraser* upheld the disciplining of the student's profane nominating speech based on the school's need to teach students about appropriate societal behavior; furthermore, the Court found that the school had wide latitude in determining the "manner of speech" that was permissible on school grounds. In the instant case, however, the school is not attempting to regulate the "manner of speech." For example, a student would be permitted to attend class wearing a T-shirt with a flag on it if the flag was in support of the country's Olympic team. As a result, it is the content of speech, not the manner, [which] the Madison County School Board wishes to regulate. In addition, a clear underpinning of the Court's holding in *Fraser* was the disruptive nature of the plaintiff's nominating speech and the fact that the sanctions were not based on one particular political viewpoint. Assuming that there has not been any racially motivated violence or threat in the Madison County schools, the plaintiffs' display of the Confederate flag may not have had any significant disruptive effect. The defendants do claim that prior to the plaintiffs' suspension, there was a racially based altercation on school grounds, but plaintiffs contend that race was not the cause of the disturbance. This disagreement simply highlights the need for a trial to determine the precise facts of this situation. . . .

The Madison County School Board's actions cannot be judged using the more lenient *Hazelwood* standard because the special circumstances present in *Hazelwood* are so clearly absent in Madison County. Castorina and Dargavell's actions were not school sponsored, nor did the school supply any of the resources involved in their wearing the T-shirts. Most importantly, no reasonable observer could conclude that the school had somehow endorsed the students' display of the Confederate flag. As a result, *Tinker* is the most relevant of the three Supreme Court cases concerning school speech and sets forth the legal framework that the district court should apply to its factual findings. Using the *Tinker* standard that "silent, passive expression of opinion, unaccompanied by any disorder or disturbance on the part of petitioners" is not subject to regulation, it is clear that a formal factual finding with respect to the disturbance—if any—caused by the plaintiffs' actions is necessary before a final decision can be entered in this case.

In addition, the two Court of Appeals decisions upholding suspensions for Confederate flag displays, *Melton v. Young* (6th Cir. 1972), and *West v. Derby Unified School District No. 260* (10th Cir. 2000), satisfy *Tinker* in ways that the Madison County suspension does not. In *West*, junior high school student T.W. drew a picture of a Confederate flag during his math class, thus violating the school's "Racial Harassment and Intimidation" policy. He was subsequently suspended and brought suit challenging the constitutionality of his punishment. The Tenth Circuit upheld the suspension as a legitimate exercise of the school's authority. Though this may appear facially similar to the Madison County controversy, in *West* there had been actual fights involving racial symbols (the Confederate flag in particular) in the school district and there was no evidence that the school district enforced the Racial Harassment and Intimidation policy in a manner that favored one type of potentially racially divisive symbols over another. As a result, the Tenth Circuit's decision in *West* merely demonstrates that a school board may ban racially divisive symbols when there has been actual racially motivated violence and when the policy is enforced without viewpoint discrimination. Since the Madison County action does not appear to satisfy either one of these criteria, the Tenth Circuit decision is of limited utility in the adjudication of the case before this court. . . .

The Importance of Factual Circumstances

The foregoing discussion of the three Supreme Court and two Court of Appeals cases demonstrates the importance of the factual circumstances in school speech cases and why a remand is necessary in this case so that the district court can resolve the plaintiffs' factual assertions. If the students' claims regarding the Malcolm X–inspired clothing (i.e., that other students wore this type of clothing and were not disciplined) and their claims that there were no prior disruptive altercations as a result of Confederate flags are found credible, the court below would be required to strike down the students' suspension as a violation of their rights of free speech as set forth in *Tinker*. In addition, even if there has been racial violence that necessitates a ban on racially divisive symbols, the school does not have the authority to enforce a viewpoint-specific ban on racially sensitive symbols and not others. Conversely, if the students cannot establish their factual claims, then the principal and school board may have acted within their constitutional authority to control student activity and behavior. In either circumstance, the facts are essential to the application of the legal framework discussed herein.

Accordingly, the summary judgment is reversed and the case remanded to the district court for trial.

> "The First Amendment does not protect
> such vague and attenuated notions of
> expression—namely, self-expression
> through any and all clothing that a
> 12-year-old may wish to wear."

School Dress Codes Are Constitutional

The Circuit Court's Decision

Jeffrey S. Sutton

In 2001 lawyer Robert Blau challenged the constitutionality of Highlands Middle School's dress code, contending that it infringed his daughter Amanda's freedom of expression and dress as well as his parental right to control what she wears. In the following viewpoint, excerpted from the US Circuit Court of Appeals for the Sixth Circuit's opinion in Blau v. Fort Thomas Public School District, *Judge Jeffrey S. Sutton asserts that no such violations can be established. Sutton points out that Amanda did not wish to convey any particular message in her style of dress, and the First Amendment does not cover such vague expressions. Moreover, he insists, the claim that the dress code breached Amanda's due process rights was trivial, and local and state authorities—not parents—direct school policies. Sutton was appointed to the Sixth Circuit in 2003.*

must show that the desired conduct (e.g., the desired clothing) can fairly be described as "imbued with elements of communication," *Johnson*, which "convey[s] a particularized message" that will "be understood by those who view it," *Spence*. The Blaus have not made that showing. To rule otherwise not only would erase the requirement that expressive conduct have an identifiable message but also would risk depreciating the First Amendment in cases in which a "particularized message" does exist. . . .

The Purpose of the Dress Code

Under the traditional test for assessing restrictions on expressive conduct, a regulation will be upheld if (1) it is unrelated to the suppression of expression, (2) it "furthers an important or substantial government interest," *O'Brien*, and (3) it "does not burden substantially more speech than necessary to further [the] interest," *Turner Broad. Sys., Inc. v. FCC* (1994). The Blaus cannot satisfy this test, much less show that the dress code suppresses a "substantial" amount of protected conduct.

First, the 2001 dress code exists in spite of, not because of, its impact on speech or expressive conduct. The dress code's stated purpose is to "create unity, strengthen school spirit and pride, and focus attention upon learning and away from distractions," which is consistent with the Council's statutory mandate to implement policies that "provide an environment to enhance the students' achievement and help the school meet [its] goals." And in promulgating the dress code based on the experiences of other school districts with similar regulations, school officials thought that the regulation would "enhance school safety, improve the learning environment, promote good behavior, reduce discipline problems, improve test scores, improve children's self-respect and self-esteem, bridge socioeconomic differences between families, help eliminate stereotypes and produce a cost savings for families." Consistent with these First-Amendment-benign objectives, the dress code does not regulate any particular viewpoint but merely regulates the

PERCENTAGE OF PUBLIC SCHOOLS THAT ENFORCED A STRICT DRESS CODE

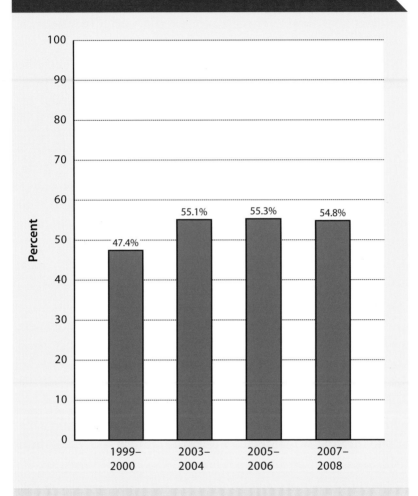

Taken from: US Department of Education, National Center on Education Statistics, 1999–2000, 2003–2004, 2005–2006, 2007–2008, School Survey on Crime and Safety (SSOCS) 2000, 2004, 2006, 2008.

types of clothes that students may wear. (The Blaus do not complain about the one seemingly content-based component of the 2001 dress code—its prohibition of any logos larger than the size of a quarter, save for Highlands logos or other "Highlands Spirit Wear.")

In response, the Blaus claim that all of this is pretext, [and] the real purpose of the code is to suppress student expression. But the only evidence the Blaus offer to bolster this contention is the statement of Highlands principal Mary Adams, who said that even though Highlands is a high-achieving school in terms of student accomplishment, it does not "mean we can't do something else to let the students know what we feel is appropriate." Merely because a dress code conveys what a school district believes is "appropriate" does not mean that the regulation exists in order to suppress speech or turns on the expressive quality of the clothing at issue. Again, the regulation is viewpoint and essentially content neutral. The only way in which a regulation of "appropriate" middle-school clothing can fairly be described as speech suppressive is if everything sartorial [of or related to clothing] is speech expressive. That is not true.

Second, the dress code furthers important governmental interests. They include: bridging socio-economic gaps between families within the school district, focusing attention on learning, increasing school unity and pride, enhancing school safety, promoting good behavior, reducing discipline problems, improving test scores, improving children's self-respect and self-esteem, helping to eliminate stereotypes and producing a cost savings for families. These are all important governmental interests, and the Blaus do not contend otherwise. . . .

Nor, under the final *O'Brien* inquiry, does the dress code suppress substantially more expressive conduct than is necessary to further its interests. As an initial matter, the Blaus have offered few examples of ways in which the dress code affects cognizable expressive conduct—except, as noted at oral argument, that the code limits the ability of students to wear t-shirts expressing their interests in music, the arts or politics. Beyond this, however, the dress code applies only to middle-school students during school hours; they remain free to dress as they (and their parents) wish in the evenings and on the weekends. And to the extent the dress code curbs expressive activity during the school day, the students have other outlets of expression during school hours: They may write for the school newspaper (which Amanda to her credit has done); they may express themselves by joining other extra-curricular activities; they may express themselves through school assignments; they may associate with whomever they (and their parents) please; and they may still wear buttons expressing other viewpoints, as permitted by the dress code. In the end, the school district has satisfied all three prongs of the *O'Brien* test, which necessarily establishes that the Blaus have not met their burden of showing that they are entitled to "the strong medicine of over breadth invalidation," *Virginia v. Hicks. . . .*

Blue Jeans and the Fourteenth Amendment

The Blaus next argue that the dress code's prohibition on blue jeans violates Amanda's substantive due process rights under the Fourteenth Amendment. We disagree.

The first (and often last) issue in this area is the proper characterization of the individual's asserted right. Governmental actions that infringe a fundamental right receive strict scrutiny. Otherwise, they receive rational-basis review, which requires them only to be "rationally related to a legitimate state interest."

Amanda faces an uphill battle in claiming that strict scrutiny applies. The list of fundamental rights "is short," it does not include the wearing of dungarees and "the Supreme Court has expressed very little interest in expanding" the list. Nor do the fundamental rights that the Court has recognized offer a flattering analogy to Amanda's claim. Whether it be the right to marry, the right to have children, the right to direct the educational upbringing of one's child, the right to marital privacy, the right to use contraception, the right to bodily integrity or the right to abortion, none of these fundamental rights has much, if anything, in common with the right to wear blue jeans. And the Court has expressly counseled lower courts to be "reluctant to expand the concept of substantive due process because guideposts for decision making in this unchartered area are scarce and open-ended." If bans on blue jeans today lie beyond the field of democratically enacted laws, in other words, what next? And by what measure of inclusion or exclusion? The Blaus have offered no explanation why "the arena of public opinion and legislative action," or its equivalent (a school board), is ill-equipped to handle the question whether blue jeans ought to be worn in public schools. . . .

The Fundamental Right of Parents

Robert Blau next argues that the dress code interferes with his fundamental right to direct the education of his child. We again disagree.

For some time and for considerably longer than most individual constitutional rights have existed, the Supreme Court has recognized a "fundamental right of parents to make decisions concerning the care, custody and control of their children," *Troxel v. Granville* (2000). And while this right plainly extends to the public school setting, it is not an unqualified right.

The critical point is this: While parents may have a fundamental right to decide whether to send their child to a public school, they do not have a fundamental right generally to direct how a public school teaches their child. Whether it is the school curriculum, the hours of the school day, school discipline, the timing and content of examinations, the individuals hired to teach at the school, the extracurricular activities offered at the school or, as here, a dress code, these issues of public education are generally "committed to the control of state and local authorities," *Goss v. Lopez* (1975). . . .

Robert Blau does not have a fundamental right to exempt his child from the school dress code.

> *"A school focusing on its responsibility to train good citizens will recognize enforcing a dress code is an important training opportunity for the student."*

School Dress Codes Improve Student Behavior

Mike Knox

Mike Knox is an expert on gangs and author of Gangsta in the House: Understanding Gang Culture. *In the following viewpoint, he contends that strictly enforced dress codes are an effective tool in teaching discipline and adherence to social standards, psychologically preparing students for academic performance and work. School uniforms are ideal, Knox asserts, have financial benefits for families, and are proven to reduce violence, misconduct, and distractions at schools. But the typical dress code has been reduced to a "cannot wear list" that requires great effort to maintain and risks litigation from parents, therefore most schools treat such violations as minor, he claims.*

Some people think of discipline as punishment. Punishment is one facet of discipline but it is not the whole. Discipline is about reward. One can reward positive or negative behavior. A true disciplinarian understands how to encourage a person to repeat positive behavior through positive reward and how to discourage unwanted behavior using negative reward. The consistent application of firm and fair discipline produces a solid foundation on which a child can build a successful pattern of behavior, which will allow the child to learn.

The earlier in a child's education career this foundation is said, the sooner the child can begin exploring and learning new life skills. Each child who begins school comes from a different family with a different set of social mores and values. Standardization of conduct is essential to the success of an individual in a culture. If a person's conduct falls outside the standard, in any society, they are ostracized, marginalized, or perhaps criminalized by that society and are prohibited from achieving success. Each child needs to begin the process of recognizing that school, and later society, are not the same as their family. In order to be successful the child must accept and adhere to certain standards. One very simple method of teaching this valuable early lesson has been, for the most part, abandoned by public schools. The controversy of the dress code exists because most do not recognize it as a teaching tool.

What Is a Dress Code?

Simply stated, a dress code is a rule promulgated by an authority to promote the desired attention to detail, to present a particular image, and to eliminate unproductive distraction from the task at hand. Every company, corporation, business, profession, vocation, or job, on the planet earth requires some type of dress code. All schools profess to have a dress code as well. The difference is, in the real world dress codes are regularly and routinely enforced.

For example, if you work for a fast food restaurant and fail to appear for work in a proper uniform, you will not work there very long. An attorney who comes dressed for the beach to a stockholders meeting, or consultation with an important client, will likewise not be employed long. Would you feel good about paying your plumber who wears a $5,000.00 Armani suit to work on your plumbing? Even exotic dancers have a . . . well, an un-dress code. In short, society expects individual[s] to "dress for success" in their field of endeavor.

The only places where dress codes are routinely ignored are public educational facilities. The public school is in an admit-tedly awkward position because they cannot fire their students. Add to this difficulty, parents who will not support the school if it decides to discipline a child for a dress code violation and in fact, may become litigious over the issue. The consequence? Academic oriented school officials see dress code violations as a minor issue and not worth the trouble.

The prevailing view is that as long as students do their home-work and produce academically, or more importantly on state mandated achievement tests, what difference does it make how they are dressed? Teachers and administrations come to view the issue of dress as a tool to control the activities of those who rebel against the academic culture of school. The dress code is quickly reduced to a simple punishment tool, often used in a sporadic and arbitrary way. The evidence of this philosophy is clear in the nature of the published dress codes of most public educational facilities.

Typical school dress codes have become "cannot wear lists." These lists are attempts to prevent students from dressing in a sexually inappropriate manner, to prevent the display of disrup-tive ideas such as racism, gang violence, drugs, alcohol, and other offensive displays designed to cause offense.

The problem with these kinds of lists is they require a great deal of maintenance. The list must be updated repeatedly, as stu-dents find creative ways to alter their clothing to express inap-propriate ideas or messages using methods of dress or accessories not prohibited by the cannot wear list.

An Important Teaching Tool

One classic example is a school that bans the use of blue or red col-ored bandanas. The school wants to prevent gang violence on and around the campus and buys into the "out of sight, out of mind" theory. In other words, if no bandanas are seen there will be no gangs on campus. It is convenient for the school administrators but not necessarily conducive to educating the offending child. Typically, such a ban does nothing to eliminate gangs on campus.

Those gang members who continue to wear the offending items are targeted for discipline and ultimately removed from the campus for a short period of time. Typically gang members simply decide to alter their identifier to some other item not banned by the school. For instance instead of bandanas, they may decide to wear blue or red beads laced into their tennis shoes, or hair, to indicate their affiliation. Now the school has to ban colored beads. Gang members simply adjust their emblems of membership each time the school bans an item. The cycle continues and becomes quite tedious.

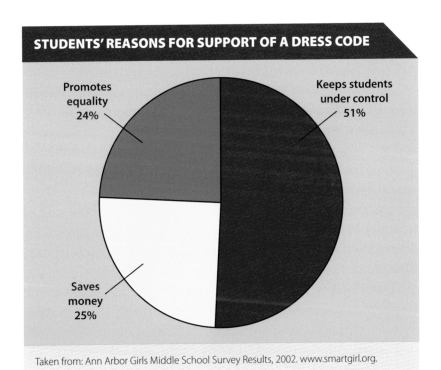

STUDENTS' REASONS FOR SUPPORT OF A DRESS CODE

Promotes equality 24%

Keeps students under control 51%

Saves money 25%

Taken from: Ann Arbor Girls Middle School Survey Results, 2002. www.smartgirl.org.

The school expends way too much time and energy attempting to enforce an increasingly ponderous set of regulations. The staff and administration become weary of fighting a never-ending battle and violations begin to be overlooked. Finally, the dress code is only invoked in "special cases" for the convenience of the administration, i.e. documenting rules violations in preparation for suspension or expulsion of particularly disruptive students. The dress code has become an arbitrary enforcement tool and completely ineffective for its original purpose to promote education.

A well written, easily enforceable, unchanging dress code, which can be effectively used in any public school environment, requires an adjustment in the perception or public education goals. Rather than a list of potential violations, a proper dress code should be constructed around the idea that the dress code is an important teaching tool.

A school focusing on its responsibility to train good citizens will recognize enforcing a dress code is an important training opportunity for the student. The dress code, in such a school, becomes a continuation of a school's commitment to educating and training students to be successful in the real world.

Schools subscribing to the citizenship-training model recognize dress standards are an integral part of the work force, in which these students will be expected to participate someday, and it is not, therefore, unreasonable for the school to acclimate their students to this concept. Parents of students attending these kinds of schools are educated as well about the necessity and importance of the dress code. Both students and parents should be told why violations will not be tolerated. Typically, parents are relieved to have an ally they can use to assist them in moderating their child's appearance.

Occasionally a parent will argue their child should be allowed to express themselves creatively through their clothing choices. One successful argument, in defense of the dress code, is to agree with the parent that self-expression is important and that the parent should encourage the child to express themselves, with clothing, to their heart's content, after school. However, the school has a responsibility to teach children skills for success. One very important work skill is the ability to accept and adhere to standardized rules of conduct and appearance.

Perhaps the most important benefit of a quality dress code is psychological. We all dress differently depending on our goals. We do not dress for recreation when we go to work and we do not dress for work when we are involved in recreation.

If a child dresses to attend school in the same clothing they would wear to play, they are not preparing, psychologically, to work. Requiring a student to dress substantially different while attending school is to train the child about the importance of dress in the work place. The child begins to associate the dress standard at school with academic work, mentally focusing on attending school, as opposed to recreational socializing. Later, they will be prepared to habitually dress for success in the workplace.

Effective Dress Codes Are Possible

A successful dress code should be very specific and leave little to personal interpretation by the student or adult. The effective dress code should clearly state the manner in which the clothing shall be worn and should apply to both male and female students.

The dress code should clearly state the acceptable style and material of shirts, pants, shorts, or dresses and should prohibit any item of clothing with advertising or slogans, including name brand identifiers. The only exception to the prohibition of name brands, logos or messages, would be those items with school logos or symbols of the school attended by the child, which have been approved by the school administration.

Personally, I recommend a unisex approach to dress codes, as the variety of feminine attire is staggering and requires a great deal of energy to enforce. Further by eliminating the dress and skirt from the school dress code, modesty regulations become

Proponents of school uniforms contend they better prepare a student by teaching discipline and respect. © Nancy Honey/Photonica/Getty Images.

moot, effectively eliminating the need to define hem lengths, the amount of exposed midriff, plunging necklines, halter-tops, tube tops, and exposed undergarments.

The Ultimate Dress Code Is the School Uniform

A school uniform provides financial, physical safety, and psychological benefits to students and parents. As with any good dress code, it helps the school set the environmental focus on good behavior and citizenship.

Requiring a school uniform provides financial relief to parents, particularly in low to middle income neighborhoods. It often costs less to purchase an entire week's worth of school uniform clothes than two days worth of stylish and popular name brand clothing items.

The school uniform is an equalizer and removes the distraction of wealth competition among students. The wealthy child is dressed in the same manner as the poor student. Therefore, there is less attention to style and more attention directed toward developing relationships based on individual characteristics than on socio-economic status. Many schools report using uniforms results in a significant reduction in student against student violence, general misconduct, and the severity of rules violation among their students.

From a safety standpoint, the school uniform provides an immediate visual verification as to whether or not a school age child belongs on a particular campus. Occasionally, students, looking for trouble, will appear on another campus to seek out rivals. A school uniform permits teachers, staff, and students to quickly recognize intruders and prevent uncontested access to their school by students from other schools.

From an administrative point of view, the uniform is the most easily enforced form of dress code. Either the child is within the uniform requirement or they are not. There is little need for discussion. The standardization of clothing increases the ability of each teacher, or administrator, to effectively enforce the dress code. Consistent enforcement of the dress code quickly creates a stable environment for the student. Once mastered, students and teachers need spend little time or attention on appearance and can focus on education and training.

We all want safer schools. We want our children to learn confidence. We want their futures to be full of possibilities. Instead of focusing on the end goal perhaps we should focus more on the little details and let the larger goal take care of itself. The little detail of a well organized and enforced dress code will go a long way in helping students achieve their life goals.

> "In attempting to cloak failures in
> American public schools, an imprudent
> move, [dress codes] highlight them
> instead—thus unintentionally doing a
> great service to the public school system."

A Student Argues Against School Dress Codes As a Solution to Behavioral Problems

Personal Narrative

David P.

In the following viewpoint, David P. argues that the adoption of strict dress codes reflects the failures of public schools. He states, for example, that banning coats and hats to deter violence demonstrates that students are insufficiently educated on weapons and gangs. In addition, restricting paraphernalia related to alcohol or tobacco on campus indicates that substance abuse programs are ineffective, the author claims. Thus he recommends that schools address these problems directly, not with policies regarding student attire. When this viewpoint was published, the author was student council president at Johnston High School in Johnston, Rhode Island.

Scituate, Rhode Island, is a community that admits it is failing its students. In Findlay, Ohio, "courtesy" supersedes one's rights. These, of course, are only two of the myriad school districts which have adopted more stringent policies regarding dress codes. When the powers-that-be at the Education Department in our nation's capital prioritize the problems facing America's public schools, I am certain that the "problem" of strict dress codes doesn't make the top 10.

But strict dress codes ARE a problem, and an anomaly, in that they are useful and harmful for the same reason. In attempting to cloak failures in American public schools, an imprudent move, they highlight them instead—thus unintentionally doing a great service to the public school system. Lucky for readers, I happen to have the Findlay and Scituate policies nearby—and a highlighter to boot.

Let us first examine the new Scituate policy: "No heavy coats may be worn inside the school, and no hats, either." This was devised to ensure the safety of students, for weapons can easily be concealed in coats or hats, and some team logos printed on caps are now logos for some gangs. While Scituate should be praised for showing concern for its students, I think it must be noted that this is Scituate's way of admitting . . . that adults in the lives of students have failed to educate them sufficiently as to the dangers and pitfalls of weapons and gangs.

Let us now delve into the Findlay policy. Hats are not allowed at Findlay High, either. Why? The principal, Victoria Brian, feels that the removal of hats is "a courtesy that we seem to have forgotten." Isn't it nice that Miss Manners now has a second job besides her newspaper column? What Ms. Brian and the Findlay School Board seem to have forgotten is that they have absolutely no right to regulate attire based on their opinions and whims. Many courts would undoubtedly find this rule in violation of the First Amendment.

By far the strongest admissions of failure and the most blatant violations of First Amendment rights in both the Findlay and Scituate policies are in the form of "message and graphics" bans. The Scituate policy bans T-shirts that "carry messages that promote alcohol or drug use," while the Findlay policy bans "language or graphics pertaining to alcohol or tobacco."

The reasoning behind the Scituate policy, as stated by Superintendent Allen G. Brown, is as follows: "We spend thousands of dollars to prevent substance abuse, and promoting alcohol is very contrary to the message we're trying to send."

Admitting Failure

With all due respect to Mr. Brown, it seems to me that this school system is admitting failure and is effectively conceding that students have obviously not grasped the perils of alcohol abuse. Once again, this is Scituate's (and perhaps Findlay's) way of saying, "Sorry, we failed."

Examining this ban from a legal standpoint, I cannot see how language, which is not obscene, can be banned. Call me a future ACLU [American Civil Liberties Union] leader, but isn't that crossing the line from concern for the health and welfare of students to pure, unadulterated censorship? Absolutely. Furthermore, according to the ACLU publication *The Right of Students*, "[Some courts] have . . . balanced the rights of the student against the need of the school to make reasonable health and safety regulations." Consequently, a policy banning hats for fear of concealed weapons is legitimate, but a "Miss Manners" policy is illegal, as is a "message and graphics" ban. And that is the way it should be.

To be sure, not all communities feel the need to infringe on their pupils' rights. Recently, Johnston High School's student leaders were asked to revise the statement of policy regarding student attire. (Involving students in policies that directly affect them? What a novel idea!) As Student Council President, I presided over the revision. Our policy has no "bans," and is one page of RECOMMENDATIONS. The last paragraph asks that "students and parents . . . use good taste and show responsibility in selecting school attire."

Does this mean that someone may enter Johnston High this year wearing a "Budweiser" shirt without fear of being disciplined? Absolutely. Might the wearing of the shirt indicate that some students are not listening to what is being taught in Johnston schools about alcohol abuse? Possibly. But such a situation will most likely make instructors work just that much harder to attempt to curb the indiscriminate use of alcohol. And it won't violate anyone's rights.

Scituate and Findlay are wearing sunglasses to keep out the rays of realism telling them that they have problems in their schools that far transcend T-shirts. One day soon those sunglasses will have to come off. After all, Scituate bans those, also.

> "Uniforms and dress codes become a
> further step in authoritarian control,
> and students forced to express
> themselves by resisting such policies are
> labeled 'troublemakers.'"

School Dress Codes Repress Students of Color

Enrique C. Ochoa

Enrique C. Ochoa is a history and Latin American studies professor at California State University, Los Angeles, and board member of the Coalition of Human Immigrant Rights Los Angeles (CHIRLA). In the following viewpoint, Ochoa claims that dress codes are part of a "hidden curriculum" designed to coerce students—especially of color—into compliance and conformity. Dress codes arose from education reforms based on testing and standards, leading to authoritarian practices in public education, he says. This emphasis on controlling the behavior of students through clothing restrictions and other policies, Ochoa contends, criminalize youth and undermine critical thinking and democratic participation.

Each new school year, a familiar battle. Last September [in 2007], our son came home upset from his second day in the eighth grade. The vice principal told him that t-shirts with messages on them, such as the ones he wears daily, would soon be banned. This was the latest in a series of run-ins we have had with the schools about my son's t-shirts, his hair styles and his denunciation of the war in Iraq in a class assignment. I called the vice principal, who defended the policy, arguing that such t-shirts disrupt school business and some even encourage graffiti and other inappropriate activity.

At a school nearby, students were subjected to random searches. Police officers and the vice principal came into the classes, interrupting the day's lessons, and made students open up backpacks and empty pockets. The violation of the classroom space had to have sent a powerful message to the students, who are overwhelmingly Latina/o. Are these same searches being carried out at middle-class schools?

Policing Youth in Communities of Color

These incidents are part of a much deeper process of policing youth in communities of color. School practices in urban areas have historically worked to create compliant subjects who "know their place" as good workers in the society. School segregation, "Americanization programs," inadequate classroom funding, school tracking and "zero-tolerance" policies are part of this history. The misplaced priorities of society and schools are overly concerned with controlling student behavior, not with educating youth as critical thinkers in a democratic society.

Sociologist David Brunsma studied effects of uniform policies extensively and concluded that they do not impact school discipline or academic achievement, are largely symbolic and reinforce a "hidden curriculum" of coercion and compliance aimed at working-class students of color.

The emphasis on discipline and control is symptomatic of a larger approach to youth of color. No Child Left Behind (NCLB) and the testing craze have translated into increased pressure on teachers and students to stay on task and follow the prescribed curriculum, with little opportunity for exploring interesting tan-

Random searches of student lockers along with strictly enforced dress codes create an environment of forced conformity and compliance some argue. © AP Images/Emily Saunders.

gents or engaging in hands-on activities. The gains of the civil rights struggles of the '60s and '70s for more relevant curriculum and bilingual education have been all but erased in this era of "standards" and testing.

NCLB has bolstered the role of public education in teaching conformity and restricted the system's role in developing participatory democratic values. The classroom pressures to "perform" often lead to more authoritarian school practices. Instead of dialoguing with students, policies are mandated and students are "talked at." Schools should be spaces for participatory democracy where students develop themselves as critical and thoughtful human beings.

Dress code and other authoritarian policies are counterproductive and a detriment to learning. In the controlled school environment, dress and appearance often are among the few spaces for creativity and individuality. Uniforms and dress codes become a further step in authoritarian control, and students forced to express themselves by resisting such policies are labeled "troublemakers." The emphasis on controlling behavior, profiling students based on race, police officers on campus, random searches, all lead to the criminalization of youth. These are the real lessons being taught to youth of color.

Subtractive Schooling

It seems that school, especially for the working classes and communities of color, is about training students to fit into a prescribed mold, follow blindly and be good consumers. All too often, schools are practicing what scholar Angela Valenzuela has referred to as "subtractive schooling," which aims at taking away students' home culture and knowledge, not building on it. While many educators and students are resisting this narrow notion of education, repressive policies dominate the structure of education. Little wonder that Latina/os and African-Americans are "pushed out" of high school at high rates and never make it to university.

Education should be about inclusive learning, participatory democracy, critical thought and self-actualization. This requires increased funding in schools, smaller classes and a curriculum relevant to the students' backgrounds and the world around them. Parents, students and teachers must work together to chart out a community-based critical democratic education. Acts of school repression have no place in a system that seeks to foster critical students who see the relevance of education, excel at the university and contribute to the creation of a socially just society.

> "The most genuine portrayal of a school's
> image is what its students achieve in
> and out of the classroom—not what
> they're wearing while doing it."

A Student Argues Against Dress Codes at Colleges and Universities

Personal Narrative

Jonathan Wright

In the following viewpoint, Jonathan Wright criticizes the use of dress codes to maintain the public image of a college or university. As a graduate of a private school where clothing policies were strictly enforced, Wright views dress codes in higher education as a form of parenting rather than real-world preparation. Instead, students should uphold the legacies of their colleges and universities through their academic and professional achievements, he suggests. Originally from Memphis, Tennessee, the author was a senior at the University of Pennsylvania when this viewpoint was published.

If you're like me and attended private school before coming to Philly, you probably were told how much facial hair was appropriate, how much jewelry you could wear or what type of clothing was acceptable for school. Thankfully, college life at Penn has afforded me the opportunity to grow a pretty incredible goatee and assemble a closet reflective of my personal style. For young men, wearing inappropriate T-shirts and getting the urge to grow that Abe Lincoln beard out of your system is part of what college is about, after all.

That is, unless you attend Morehouse College in Atlanta. The historically-black institution and alma mater of Martin Luther King, Jr. has implemented an "Appropriate Attire Policy" that prohibits members of its all-male student body from wearing clothing featuring lewd messages or pictures, baseball caps inside school venues or class, and jeans during major school programs, among other regulations. Although many other schools have dress codes, Morehouse's policy is distinctive because it's solely based on what's not acceptable, not what is approved clothing.

While administrations at private institutions unquestionably have the authority to set guidelines for students that coincide with the vision or image of their schools, a dress code for college students—and a restriction-based one at that—seems more like parenting than preparation for the real world.

Critics of dress codes point out that they focus on superficial matters and don't necessarily impact learning—something even truer at colleges, where students don't stay with the same cohort all day. And while we need to understand workplace attire before graduation, Intro to Sociology is hardly the place for that lesson.

But Morehouse isn't citing these traditional motives. In an article detailing the school's new policy in *The Maroon Tiger*, the school newspaper, there is no mention of professionalism, preparing students for corporate America or improving academic performance. The article does, however, mention the "college's outstanding legacy of producing leaders" and the school's expectation that students dress "neatly and appropriately at all times."

Constraining Personal Expression

The impressive list of alumni and accomplishments the school has achieved over the years speaks for itself. And I don't know much about being a Morehouse Man, but I find it difficult to imagine that a student could tarnish the school's legacy by wearing a Yankees cap during lunch. Sure, I've heard that King and his classmates wore suits during their years there, but times have changed. It's unfair to connect the legacy that King—along with those who preceded and followed him—left at Morehouse with what the students of this era deem trendy or stylish.

But any gripe that I have with the policy is negligible, if Morehouse students agree with Cameron Thomas-Shah, co-chairman of the Student Government Association. Thomas-Shah supports the move and echoed the administration's stance on the school's legacy.

"Morehouse College has a very strong image to uphold," he wrote in an e-mail, adding that the students are charged with "maintaining an appropriate image of the college for the sake of sustainability and growth." I don't disagree with him about the students' responsibility to maintain a school's image, but the most genuine portrayal of a school's image is what its students achieve in and out of the classroom—not what they're wearing while doing it.

Granted, as a collective student body we may face different issues or represent different values than Morehouse. But besides a few questionable (ok, downright tacky) ensembles thrown together by our classmates occasionally, most of us here would agree that a University dress code that seeks to uphold Penn's image and legacy would be unnecessary—not because the name "Penn" speaks for itself. But we've been afforded the opportunity to see that professional development and educational achievement don't have to constrain personal expression in any way. We've got the rest of our lives to uphold the Penn legacy. We've only got four years to wear immature t-shirts.

> *"Public school students who may be
> injured by verbal assaults on the basis of
> a core identifying characteristic . . . have
> a right to be free from such attacks
> while on school campuses."*

Schools May Restrict Expression on Clothing That Attacks Other Students

The Circuit Court's Decision

Stephen Roy Reinhardt

In 2004, Tyler Chase Harper, a California high school student, was ordered by administrators to remove the anti-gay message on his shirt and prevented from attending class when he refused. In the following viewpoint, excerpted from the US Circuit Court of Appeals for the Ninth Circuit's opinion in Harper v. Poway Unified School District, *Judge Stephen Roy Reinhardt affirms the district court's denial of a preliminary injunction for Harper on the basis that he impinged on others' rights and, in the circumstances presented, did not meet the* Tinker *standard of free speech. According to Reinhardt, Harper may lawfully be prohibited from wearing the shirt because its message was substantially disruptive—conflicts involving sexual orientation had already taken place on campus—*

Stephen Roy Reinhardt, *Harper v. Poway Unified School District*, Findlaw.com, April 20, 2006. Copyright © 2006 by Findlaw Inc. All rights reserved. Reproduced by permission.

and discriminatory toward homosexual students. Reinhardt was appointed to the Ninth Circuit in 1980.

May a public high school prohibit students from wearing T-shirts with messages that condemn and denigrate other students on the basis of their sexual orientation? Appellant in this action is a sophomore at Poway High School who was ordered not to wear a T-shirt to school that read, "BE ASHAMED, OUR SCHOOL EMBRACED WHAT GOD HAS CONDEMNED" handwritten on the front, and "HOMOSEXUALITY IS SHAMEFUL" handwritten on the back.

He appeals the district court's order denying his motion for a preliminary injunction. Because he is not likely to succeed on the merits, we affirm the district court's order. . . .

Freedom of Speech Claim

The district court concluded that [Tyler Chase] Harper failed to demonstrate a likelihood of success on the merits of his claim that the School violated his First Amendment right to free speech because, under *Tinker v. Des Moines Indep. Cmty. Sch. Dist.*, the evidence in the record was sufficient to permit the school officials to "reasonably forecast substantial disruption of or material interference with school activities." Harper contends that the district court erred in rejecting his free speech claim on three grounds: (1) his speech is protected under the Supreme Court's holdings in *Tinker* and *Bethel Sch. Dist. v. Fraser* (1986); (2) the School's actions and policies amount to viewpoint discrimination under *Rosenberger v. Rector & Visitors of Univ. of Va.* (1995); and (3) the School's dress code and speech policies are overbroad under *Bd. of Airport Comm'rs of Los Angeles v. Jews for Jesus* (1987). We affirm the district court's denial of the requested preliminary injunction. Although we, like the district court, rely on *Tinker*, we rely on a different provision—that schools may prohibit speech that "intrudes upon the rights of other students."

Student Speech Under *Tinker*

Public schools are places where impressionable young persons spend much of their time while growing up. They do so in order to receive what society hopes will be a fair and full education—an education without which they will almost certainly fail in later life, likely sooner rather than later. The public school, with its free education, is the key to our democracy. Almost all young Americans attend public schools. During the time they do—from first grade through twelfth—students are discovering what and who they are. Often, they are insecure. Generally, they are vulnerable to cruel, inhuman, and prejudiced treatment by others.

The courts have construed the First Amendment as applied to public schools in a manner that attempts to strike a balance between the free speech rights of students and the special need to maintain a safe, secure and effective learning environment. This court has expressly recognized the need for such balance: "States have a compelling interest in their educational system, and a balance must be met between the First Amendment rights of students and preservation of the educational process," *LaVine v. Blaine Sch. Dist.* (9th Cir. 2001). Although public school students do not "shed their constitutional rights to freedom of speech or expression at the schoolhouse gate," *Tinker*, the Supreme Court has declared that "the First Amendment rights of students in public schools are not automatically coextensive with the rights of adults in other settings, and must be applied in light of the special characteristics of the school environment," *Hazelwood Sch. Dist. v. Kuhlmeier* (1988). Thus, while Harper's shirt embodies the very sort of political speech that would be afforded First Amendment protection outside of the public school setting, his rights in the case before us must be determined "in light of [those] special characteristics" *Tinker*.

This court has identified "three distinct areas of student speech," each of which is governed by different Supreme Court precedent: (1) vulgar, lewd, obscene, and plainly offensive speech which is governed by *Fraser*, (2) school-sponsored speech, which is governed by *Hazelwood*, and (3) all other speech, which is governed by *Tinker*.

In *Tinker*, the Supreme Court confirmed a student's right to free speech in public schools. In balancing that right against the state interest in maintaining an ordered and effective public education system, however, the Court declared that a student's speech rights could be curtailed under two circumstances. First, a school may regulate student speech that would "impinge upon the rights of other students." Second, a school may prohibit student speech that would result in "substantial disruption of or material interference with school activities." Because, as we explain below, the School's prohibition of the wearing of the demeaning T-shirt is constitutionally permissible under the first of the *Tinker* prongs, we conclude that the district court did not abuse its discretion in finding that Harper failed to demonstrate a likelihood of success on the merits of his free speech claim.

The Rights of Other Students

In *Tinker*, the Supreme Court held that public schools may restrict student speech which "intrudes upon the rights of other students" or "colli[des] with the rights of other students to be secure and to be let alone." Harper argues that *Tinker's* reference to the "rights of other students" should be construed narrowly to involve only circumstances in which a student's right to be free from direct physical confrontation is infringed. Drawing on the Fifth Circuit's opinion in *Blackwell v. Issaquena County Bd. of Ed.* (5th Cir. 1966), which the Supreme Court cited in *Tinker*, Harper contends that because the speakers in *Blackwell* "accosted other students by pinning the buttons on them even though they did not ask for one," a student must be physically accosted in order to have his [or her] rights infringed.

Photo on next page: The circuit court's decision states that a school can ban messages on T-shirts that attack a student's sexual orientation. © AP Images/Karen Tam.

est in providing a proper educational environment for its students, and because its actions were narrowly tailored to achieve that end, it would appear that the district court did not abuse its discretion in finding that Harper failed to demonstrate a likelihood of success on the merits as to his free exercise of religion claim. Before reaching that conclusion, however, we must deal with one final argument that Harper raises as a part of that claim. Harper asserts that the School "attempted to change" his religious views that "homosexuality is harmful to both those who practice it and the community at large." Specifically, Harper alleges that the school officials' comments that his shirt was "inflammatory," Detective [Norman] Hubbert's questioning of him, and Assistant Principal [Ed] Giles' statement that he leaves his Christian faith in the car when he comes to school, all were attempts by school authorities to change his religious views.

The district court rejected Harper's contention. Indeed, there is no evidence in the record that the school representatives sought to change Harper's religious beliefs. Harper's complaint avers that Detective Hubbert "proposed to [Harper] that as a member of the Christian faith, he should understand that Christianity was based on love not hate, and that [he] should not be offensive to others." Hubbert's homily did not constitute an attempt to change Harper's religious views, simply his offensive behavior; at most, it was, as the district court concluded, an "option presented to and left with" Harper. The statements that the message on Harper's shirt was "inflammatory" and would be harmful to the educational environment were merely statements of fact that represented the School's informed judgment. More important, like Hubbert's statement, they were designed to affect Harper's behavior not his beliefs. As for Giles' comments, his affidavit stated that he did not tell Harper to "leave his own faith in the car," but explained that, as a school employee, he, Giles, had to leave his own Christian faith in the car when he came to work. While Giles' statement might also be construed as an attempt to encourage Harper to change his conduct—to refrain, while on campus, from expressing religious views that denigrate others—it cannot be characterized as an attempt to change his views. In fact, rather than tell Harper to change his beliefs, Giles encouraged him to join the campus Bible Club so that he could become part of an "activity that would express his [Christian] opinions in a positive way on campus," an activity that was wholly consistent with Harper's religious views. The record thus does not support Harper's claim that the School violated his free exercise right by "attempting to change" his religious views.

Moreover, school officials' statements and any other school activity intended to teach Harper the virtues of tolerance constitute a proper exercise of a school's educational function, even if the message conflicts with the views of a particular religion. A public school's teaching of secular democratic values does not constitute an unconstitutional attempt to influence students' religious beliefs. Rather, it simply reflects the public school's performance of its duty to educate children regarding appropriate secular subjects in an appropriate secular manner. As we have reiterated earlier, "the inculcation of fundamental values necessary to the maintenance of a democratic political system" is "truly the 'work of the schools.'" Public schools are not limited to teaching materials that are consistent with all aspects of the views of all religions. So long as the subject and materials are appropriate from an educational standpoint and the purpose of the instruction is secular, the school's teaching is not subject to a constitutional objection that it conflicts with a view held by members of a particular religion. There is no evidence here that the school officials' comments were associated with a religious, as opposed to a secular, purpose. Their affidavits demonstrate that the School acted in order to maintain a secure and healthy learning environment for all its students, not to advance religion. . . .

We hold that the district court did not abuse its discretion in denying the preliminary injunction.

Harper failed to demonstrate that he will likely prevail on the merits of his free speech, free exercise of religion, or establishment of religion claims. In fact, such future success on Harper's part is highly unlikely, given the legal principles discussed in this opinion. The Free Speech Clause permits public schools to restrict student speech that intrudes upon the rights of other students. Injurious speech that may be so limited is not immune from regulation simply because it reflects the speaker's religious views. Accordingly, we affirm the district court's denial of Harper's motion for a preliminary injunction.

> "School uniforms can bring back a
> little bit more respect for teachers and
> students in the classroom."

Uniforms in Public Schools Are Beneficial

Angela Walmsley

Angela Walmsley is associate dean for graduate education and research in the College of Education and Public Service at Saint Louis University in Missouri. In the following viewpoint, she claims that requiring uniforms is a reasonable and effective way to enhance the school environment for students and faculty alike. Drawing from her teaching experience in a British school, Walmsley suggests that the presence of uniforms instills a sense of duty and focus in students, creating more respect for teachers and safer campuses. Uniforms are also less expensive than trendy or brand-name clothing, she continues, and free administrators from the time-consuming enforcement of dress codes.

Students walk the school hallways in an orderly fashion, dressed professionally in uniforms consisting of blazers with the school's crest and skirts for girls and trousers for boys. They don't walk with hands in their pockets. Students are polite and wait for the teacher outside the classroom door. When he says to enter, all students enter and stand at their desks until everyone is inside. They don't sit until the teacher invites them to sit. Students prepare for their lesson and are, for the most part, quite content and respectful. Where am I?

This description sounds like it might be from a wealthy preparatory school, but instead it's a regular state school in England where school tradition and respect are among the school's goals for children. Two-thirds of the students come from the surrounding low-income area, but these children look like a picture from a wealthy New England prep school. Students have a range of abilities, but they all share one thing in common: respect for the teachers, the school, and themselves.

How does a school create this type of culture? I believe part of it is from the presence of school uniforms.

I was never an advocate of school uniforms. Having attended a U.S. public school myself, I couldn't imagine wearing a uniform. When I taught in an American public school, I thought uniforms were significant only because they identified anyone who attended a private school. But I began to see the benefit of school uniforms when I taught in a British school a number of years ago and later when my own children attended English schools.

To understand the benefits, readers need a short background of British education. Every British school requires that students wear a school uniform. Schools choose their own required uniform, and parents are responsible for providing the uniform. Some schools may offer support or discounted items for needy children. I used to think American schools couldn't do this because schools would be required to pay for the clothing for anyone who couldn't afford it. However, because the school uniform is part of the British culture, U.K. schools do not need to provide students with the clothing. Children have a job, and that job is to attend school. Just as their parents must wear appropriate clothing for work, students must wear appropriate clothing for school. Parents are used to wearing uniforms or appropriate clothing for their own professions and this culture is passed down to their children. But the "catch" is that school uniforms in the United Kingdom are not that expensive.

Not a Costly Alternative

In the United States, most private schools that require uniforms choose a plaid or specific item that the students must buy to signal that they belong to that school. This may be costly because these items might be available only at one or two places. In the United Kingdom, schools choose "generic" items that can be bought anywhere. When every school must follow the rule, more of the items become available at lower costs. In the United Kingdom, most primary schools require boys to wear dark-gray or black trousers and a white polo shirt with a school sweatshirt; they require girls to wear dark-gray pants or skirts with tights and a white polo shirt and school sweatshirt cardigan.

This means the school item with the logo is the sweatshirt or cardigan, and all other items can be found in multiple shops in Britain. For example, a family can buy a summer jumper for about $6. Trousers cost about $12. Because of competition, uniform costs go drastically down. Parents can usually buy school-specific items through the school at a reduced cost. At a recent school fair (carnival) at my children's school, used items were about 75 cents per item.

When students attend secondary school, they usually require more formal dress. They follow the above guidelines, but a blazer or jacket replaces the school sweatshirt or cardigan. The dress code also specifies black shoes, a black backpack or bag with limited writing, and limited jewelry and makeup.

British parents generally prefer school uniforms because the cost can be less than buying multiple designer outfits. Also, there are no battles in the morning about what to wear to school—the

PRINCIPALS' VIEWS OF THE EFFECTS OF SCHOOL UNIFORMS

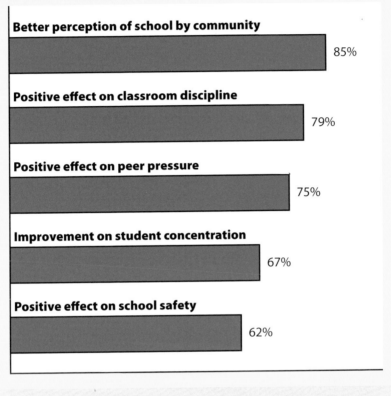

Better perception of school by community

85%

Positive effect on classroom discipline

79%

Positive effect on peer pressure

75%

Improvement on student concentration

67%

Positive effect on school safety

62%

Taken from: National Association of Elementary School Principals, "School Uniforms: Why and How," August 2000.

choice is simple. Parents appreciate needing to buy only a few shirts, a few trousers, skirts, tights, and possibly a blazer, cardigan, or sweatshirt for the entire school year. It's actually more reasonable to do this than to buy the many clothes that U.S. parents feel they must buy. As a parent with children who attended both a U.S. public school followed by a U.K. school, I know I spent less money and needed far fewer items of clothing for my children when they wore school uniforms.

Teachers appreciate the fact that the presence of school uniforms brings a sense of duty to the students and respect for the school and teachers. U.K. teachers told me they believe school uniforms help students focus on school and not each other's clothes. Because everyone looks basically the same, differences in economic status are not as blatant. Because students dress in uniforms, they're reminded that their "job" is to be a student.

Does this mean that all students behave and study all the time? Certainly not, but it's helped create a culture where students generally are proud of their school and more respectful to teachers and administrators. Also, because students are identified by their school clothing, teachers and parents can easily see who belongs in the school. This can also be helpful on field trips, in an emergency, etc.

Another issue related to school uniforms is the teacher dress code. Because schools consistently use student uniforms, U.K. schools often have a dress code for teachers. Primary teachers typically dress very professionally, but in clothing that allows them to work with children. They may wear trousers, skirts, and sometimes adult versions of the school sweatshirt. On the other hand, secondary teachers wear the more formal dress of suits or business-type clothing. Again, the school culture is affected in a positive way because teachers always look professional, and students generally treat them as professionals.

In an era when some students lack respect for teachers, the presence of school uniforms seems to automatically promote a culture of respect. This is true in the student-teacher relationship, the teacher-teacher relationship, and the parent-teacher relationship. While the United States spends time and money on the parent-teacher-student triad, the addition of school uniforms would be something simple that would strengthen this relationship.

Uniforms and Poverty

Targeting school uniforms to high-poverty areas in the United States is a mistake. While the benefits of school uniforms are reaching these schools, we're creating a culture where only the wealthiest (private schools) and poorest (high-poverty public schools) wear school uniforms. Most high-poverty schools suggest school uniforms because they believe that will reduce the threat of violence. While this seems to be working for these schools, we're creating a culture where parents think that a public school where children wear uniforms is an unsafe place to send their child. In other words, school uniforms in public schools are becoming associated with schools facing violence problems. If we want the true benefits of school uniforms to reach all children, we must create a culture where it is not only accepted but expected in all schools. . . .

Enforcing Dress Codes

Some have argued that school uniforms will never work because making a rule that requires them would not be enforceable. Many suggest that students, particularly at the high school level, would claim that they have the constitutional right to opt out. In the United States, for those schools that adopt school uniform policies, about 40% make the wearing of uniforms voluntary while 60% make wearing uniforms mandatory. My experience in the United Kingdom leads me to believe that even if the policy was voluntary, once students began wearing them, the culture would shift and most students would move toward wearing uniforms, especially if this policy is initiated in younger grades.

In the United Kingdom, most schools have a few non-uniform days each year when they raise money for charities by allowing students to donate funds in exchange for dressing as they want for the day. While many students find this fun and a good way to raise money, many secondary students still choose to wear their school uniform for the day (even if they also donate to the charity). When I've asked students why they still wear their uniform, they say they don't like "contests" that begin between students about who has the latest and greatest item of clothing. They also individually stress the importance of being a student and having

All British schools require students to wear uniforms. © John Downing/Hulton Archive/ Getty Images.

pride in the school they attend. Many of these students say dress-down days are somewhat distracting. While all of this may be true, it's amazing that so many students, after experiencing the school uniform culture, choose themselves to not opt out of the uniform policy even when given the choice.

Most U.S. schools have written dress codes. Furthermore, administrators and teachers spend considerable time addressing issues when students don't comply with the school dress code. One principal said he spends 60 to 90 minutes each day dealing with dress code issues. Compliance is easier with school uniforms because the rules are clear and, for the most part, very straightforward. When issues surrounding the dress code are diminished, there is more time for student learning.

The research concerning the academic changes and changes in the self-confidence and motivation of students who wear school uniforms in the United States is mixed. Much of the research does not support major gains in self-confidence and motivation. But that might be because much of this research is done in only poorer schools—the ones that introduce uniforms to help students avoid gang violence. A variety of schools must be analyzed in order to see if cultural change and changes in self-perception and motivation occur across a variety of students. Furthermore, almost all the research on this topic in the United States is done in elementary and middle schools. Little research on school uniforms in the United States occurred before the early 1990s, so we have had less than two decades to understand the benefits or to see school culture shift in response to school uniforms.

[Research analyst Wendell] Anderson provides four basic reasons for promoting school uniforms: 1) enhanced school safety, 2) improved learning climate, 3) higher self-esteem for students, and 4) less stress on the family. Anderson further states that when students dress alike, a "team-like" culture develops, and this promotes school spirit and positive self-images. Also, students who wear uniforms can focus on academics, rather than on what others are wearing. "Uniforms set the tone for a proper attitude towards work." This climate should also bring higher self-image and more respect for teachers.

Critics of school uniforms believe that decreases in gang violence and better school climate can be attributed to other causes and that not enough empirical evidence exists to link changes to school uniforms. While little quantitative research supports uniforms, many principals report seeing better student behavior and more concentration on school work. One must be careful not to discredit the qualitative data about school climate. If students feel more comfortable and teachers see that students are more settled and ready to learn when wearing school uniforms, then this data is solid and must be credited.

While the debate over school uniforms continues, educators must realize that school uniforms won't solve the many problems facing schools today. Instead, they should be used to create a positive school climate in which students focus on learning. School uniforms can bring back a little bit more respect for teachers and students in the classroom.

> *"I'm against school uniforms because
> it's more government, less freedom, less
> individual decision-making, and there
> is no clear link between school uniforms
> and causes of problems in schools."*

Uniforms in Public Schools Cannot Be Fairly Enforced

Clair Schwan

In the following viewpoint, Clair Schwan insists that uniforms are an ineffective "one size fits all" approach to problems in government schools. In his opinion, such policies punish the entire student body for the actions of a few and do not identify the primary causes of violence, disruptive behavior, and poor academic performance. Uniforms are also not enough to transform schools into communities of "oneness," he adds. In fact they discourage individual thinking and free expression and introduce more government into schools, Schwan suggests. Based in Cheyenne, Wyoming, the author is founder of the website Libertarian Logic.

Let's examine the arguments against school uniforms in government schools.

Despite the enthusiasm for uniforms, there are plenty of good sound reasons to avoid them. As noted in my discussion of the benefits of school uniforms in government schools, they are something that could work well for certain individuals, but the idea that "one size fits all" just isn't appealing to this Libertarian.

So let's start. Making the top of the list is the idea that this policy is a "one size" fits all, and we all know that isn't true.

This is a common and irritating approach to government. Would you like it if a retail outlet treated you like a shoplifter? Of course not, but that's exactly what a "one size fits all" approach to doing business would have your local retailers doing.

Punishing Everyone for the Actions of a Few

We should have the courage to identify bad actors and implement measures directed at them. Instead, we punish every student with a "one size fits all" mentality. If you look closely at the overall student body, you'll likely find that there is a small percentage of students that are gang members or drug dealers or miscreants of some sort.

Why not target these individuals for control measures instead of everyone? Why not target these individuals for expulsion instead of treating the entire student body as if they were a threat of some sort?

Our system of laws and regulations typically punish everyone for the actions of a few. It's always the few who ruin things for the rest of us because of our proclivity to broadly apply a rule instead of taking the time to sort out who the trouble-makers are and deal with them individually. . . .

Clothing Does Not Cause Bad Behavior

Implementing a school uniform program by itself reinforces the idea that simply changing what students wear will make a difference in their behavior. It's a type of "preventive law." A restriction that is supposed to stop some undesirable behavior.

The fact that we try it in the first place gives it some level of credibility as if student dress is really the root cause of poor behavior and lower performance in school. It's not, so it's reasonable to be against school uniforms because there isn't a cause and effect relationship—something else is causing the violence, bad behavior and poor performance.

Avoiding Proper Analysis

[A school uniform program is] an idea for fixing problems that allows us to conveniently avoid proper analysis that would identify causes of student violence and poor performance, and create appropriate solutions.

First and foremost, we need to clearly identify the problems. Then, we need to identify the immediate causes of the problems. Only then can we target "fixes" that address the causes. If we effectively address the causes, then the problems will be reduced or eliminated.

I'm against school uniforms simply because a *lack of school uniforms* isn't what's causing all the problems. . . .

A "Just Add Water" Approach

If everyone wears the same clothes, that doesn't transform individual students into wonderful community members with like minds and spirit. There needs to be more at work to create such "oneness," and it takes years to build such a culture.

This type of thinking is a typical American "drive through" and "just add water" approach that imagines such transformations could be created by quick and simple methods.

It's very much like our foreign policies, we forget about the culture of others and how that can't be changed overnight, no matter how much we wish it to be. We apparently have the same arrogance when it comes to the culture of communities and individuals.

Not the Role of Government

Requiring uniforms isn't the role of government, unless that same government organization is providing uniforms for their troops, and history shows that some countries have done just that. . . .

If we allow school officials to prescribe school uniforms, then we can expect rules on hair styles, makeup, deodorant, dental hygiene, fingernail length, shoes and so on. I don't like to let the "camel's nose under the tent," so I'm against school uniforms as a broad brush approach to solving problems. . . .

Creating More Followers than Leaders

I believe it's very likely that forcing kids to dress alike will only help create more followers than leaders. If you become accustomed to being told what to do, then how do you handle it when you finally graduate and you're placed in an environment where you're not told what to do?

Some maintain uniforms discourage individual thinking and free expression. © Lisa Pines/ Photonica/Getty Images.

I think school uniforms set some students up for failure when it comes to making their own decisions about who they are and how they're going to present themselves to the world.

If you're in favor of individual responsibility, then you're likely to be against school uniforms because such rules don't foster individuality or individual responsibility, they diminish it.

Unless you're going straight from a government school into the military, the idea of a dress code isn't the way the real world works. People in a free society dress they way they would like to. Especially in America, the melting pot, we have all manner of dress that originates from our cultural differences. I thought we were supposed to be inclusive, accepting and tolerant.

Self-Image Is Adversely Affected

Self-image can be adversely affected by forcing someone to wear something that they dislike. Just think of all the unusual clothes that some people wear—baggy pants, jackets with arms too long, long legged pants that stack up around the ankles, hats on backwards and sideways, and blue jeans that are washed out and torn at the knees. We're talking about personal choices in dress here.

Now, imagine that parents forced their kids to go to school with worn out, ripped and misfitting clothes that were placed on them backwards or inside out. This wouldn't be personal choice, but it could be viewed as quite uncalled for.

I could envision a lot of conflict arising from forcing a child to wear something they dislike. The same would be true if government officials from the school system told you how to dress, and that's why I'm against school uniforms.

If you think baggy pants allow students to bring weapons to school, then I suggest that clothes aren't the cause of weapons, it's something else. Let's focus on logical cause and effect relationships, not band-aids like school uniforms.

School uniforms diminish free expression at a time when young people are trying to establish who they are among throngs of others. There is such a thing as distractions in the classroom, but that can be handled on a case-by-case basis or with a reasonable dress code.

Punishing free expression by everyone because of the actions of a few is a bad precedence. It's not what freedom is all about.

An Additional Financial Burden

Uniforms cost money, and that's an additional financial burden placed on families. If a family would like to purchase a set of clothes for their children to wear to school—"school clothes"—then that's just fine.

Requiring a uniform to be purchased from a supplier isn't the business of school authorities, and the additional cost isn't justified. It's just another example of government mandates that aren't funded. And we can expect uniform suppliers to continually lobby our legislators and school boards to have such unfunded mandates remain in place, simply because it's in their financial interest.

You get the idea. I'm against school uniforms, and I think most freedom-minded people are too. America is strong because we are composed of individuals who are allowed to be leaders and innovators. We're strong because our government is supposed to be limited in scope and depth.

I'm against school uniforms because it's more government, less freedom, less individual decision-making, and there is no clear link between school uniforms and causes of problems in schools. I went to government schools that didn't require uniforms, and it didn't seem to affect our performance one little bit.

If you believe that a lack of school uniforms is the cause of troubles in government schools, then you'll also likely believe that disease is caused by a lack of medication. And, this begs me to repeat this important point: this Libertarian is against school uniforms because we haven't done our homework to show that trouble in school is caused by a lack of school uniforms.

> "Whether one is for making baggy
> pants illegal or not, . . . it is time young
> people of color stop imitating the prison
> lifestyle and embrace the lifestyle of
> freedom and prosperity."

Sagging Pants Should Be Banned

Todd A. Smith

In the following viewpoint, Todd A. Smith writes that wearing sagging pants embraces criminality and should not be encouraged. Smith suggests that the fad's popularity among minority youths is an invasion of prison culture, from which it originated, into mainstream America. Nonetheless, he acknowledges that outlawing sagging pants may violate civil rights, and he does not take a position on such policies and ordinances. Smith is a writer, adjunct journalism professor at Texas Southern University, and founder of Regal Magazine, *an online publication for African American men.*

In Eazy E's 1988 classic song, "We Want Eazy," former R&B sensation Michel'le asks the late rapper, "Hey Eazy, why you wear your pants like that?" His reply was, "I wear my pants like this for easy access, baby." Twenty years later with sagging pants becoming a huge fashion trend nationwide, the follow up question should be easy access for whom?

Originating from Prison Culture

The fashion trend that has become so popular in communities of color, probably as a result of the popularity and influence of the hip-hop culture, actually has its origins in prison culture.

According to Shamontiel, a blogger for *Associated Content*, "Sagging pants was never meant to be fashionable. Prisoners wear their pants this low because belts are a popular way to commit suicide by hanging oneself, to hang others, or to use as weapons in fights. Prisoners are also not allowed to have shoe-strings for the same reasons. But there is an even more obvious reason why pants are sagging in prison. If the pants are below a man's bottom, it is to introduce to other men that he is homosexual."

The sagging pants trend has become so bothersome to many that several local governments across the country have banned or attempted to ban sagging, by issuing fines and even jail time to those who show their underwear or body parts as a result of sagging. However, many opponents of the law say that these ordinances unfairly target African Americans by prohibiting them to freely express themselves through their attire.

As of August 2008, the Chicago suburb of Midlothian became the latest town to propose a law that would outlaw saggy pants that reveal rear-end cracks and underwear.

"We're not talking about someone with low-slung clothing; we're talking about when clothing is worn in such a fashion that displays body parts," said Midlothian Police Chief Vince Schavone. "It's not just pants hanging; it's if their pants are down."

Asked if sagging pants should be banned, writer Leigha Gonzales replied: "Should saggy pants come to an end? A definite yes to me. Who cares about which type of underwear are worn or what rear-end crack looks like. I assume that most individuals wear underwear whether it is a thong or boxing shorts. Everyone has a rear-end crack! Who needs to see that?"

Many communities, such as this one in Brooklyn, are trying to discourage young people from wearing sagging pants. © AP Images/Robert Mecea.

A Criminal Offense

However, some critics of sagging pants are also against making it a criminal offense and believe law enforcement should spend taxpayer dollars on initiatives that reduce crime and not those that ridicule fashion. An *Associated Content* blogger, who writes under the pen name mmog37, believes saggy trousers are just another rebellious fad for teenagers just like the jheri curl and bell bottoms, although she finds it offensive. Writer Monique Finley believes that sagging pants are tacky, especially on a job interview unless that job requires such a dress code, but believes people should be allowed to wear whatever they choose without fear of police involvement.

"It is one thing for a school to have dress codes," said Finley. "It is a whole different subject for the City (Shreveport, La.) to issue ordinances, which carry fines for citizens who are not breaking the law. Having to pull up your pants shouldn't be punishable. If you just lost weight it should be celebrated. Perhaps you can't afford new clothing. Clothing ordinances are plain and simply, a violation of citizens' rights. Business owners, government buildings, these places have the right to establish dress codes. But I should be allowed to wear my baggy jeans in my front yard without fear of police harassment."

Bizarro

Embracing Freedom and Prosperity

Nevertheless, the issue of the prison culture invading the African American culture is at the heart of the sagging pants debate. Whether one is for making baggy pants illegal or not, what should be agreed upon is the fact that it is time young people of color stop imitating the prison lifestyle and embrace the lifestyle of freedom and prosperity. So whether it's Eazy E speaking on his baggy pants in "We Want Eazy" or Run D.M.C. sporting Adidas with no shoelaces in "My Adidas," it is time that the behavior and attire of inmates are shunned and not celebrated within communities of color.

14

> *"The objection is that banning . . . baggy
> pants is inherently discriminatory, since
> they are part of a lifestyle that emerged
> out of a specific type of black culture."*

A Ban on Sagging Pants Is Discriminatory

Andrew Potter

*Andrew Potter is a columnist on culture and Canadian politics for
Maclean's. In the following viewpoint, he writes that a ban on sagging pants discriminates against black youths and attacks hip-hop
culture. While such ordinances cite public safety concerns, Potter
contends that they are a form of racial profiling similar to bans
on the zoot suits favored by African and Latino Americans in the
1930s and 1940s. The function of these dress-code laws is to reinforce the aesthetic tastes and morals of the dominant society, he asserts, and the conformity in style among all social classes from the
mid-1960s and before reflects a repressive mass culture.*

What are we to make of the growing campaign against hip-
hop streetwear? Last week [in September 2007], the city
of Atlanta introduced an ordinance that would ban baggy trousers that show boxer shorts (for guys) or low-slung jeans that
reveal thong straps (for girls). In doing so, it became the latest

in a lengthening string of political jurisdictions and private institutions, in the United States and the U.K., that have moved to police gangsta fashion using what amount to dress codes.

Often, the pretext for the ban is public safety. When Imperial College London banned hoodies from its campus back in 2005, college officials spun it as a matter of security. The ban, which included hijabs, was directed at any clothing that obscured an individual's face and interfered with the ability of security guards to match a person's face to the photo on their ID card. Similarly, part of the rhetoric against baggy pants is that their capacious pockets and tremendous folds of cloth make it all too easy to conceal knives, guns, drugs, and other illegal paraphernalia.

There is no question that, in the upside-down status signalling of urban street theatre, the point of wearing gangsta gear is to convey the message that you are a criminal. Nothing says "I've been to prison" like having lost your belt and shoelaces, while every drug dealer knows that the trick to keeping warm while selling dime bags on a cold street corner is to dress in layers—a do-rag under a hoodie, with a big puffy coat on top.

But at some point, a legitimate concern for safety turns into the official harassment of a minority underclass—or perhaps of poseurs laying claim to that identity—and it is not always easy to know where one trips into the other. As an example of an easy case, residents of Harlem were justifiably outraged a few weeks ago when local retailers started stocking a line of New York Yankees caps in gang colours like Bloods red and Crips blue. In Harlem, wearing (or not wearing) one of these colours in the wrong place can get you killed, and only after a street protest by community activists did the manufacturer agree to pull the caps from store shelves.

More often than not, though, a style or type of clothing is targeted for reasons that are more about public morals rather than public safety. The sponsor of the Atlanta ordinance, city councillor C.T. Martin, more or less admitted as much when he proposed it as an amendment to the city's indecency laws. Since that would be the same part of the municipal code that bans having sex or masturbating in public, Atlanta has set itself the rather bizarre proposition of preparing to treat wannabe Fiddies [rapper 50 Cent] or Xtinas [singer Christina Aguilera] as equivalent to subway flashers and exhibitionists.

Descendants of Older Laws

Thus, it is hardly surprising that many people oppose the introduction of these sorts of dress-code laws on the grounds that they are just racial profiling masquerading as a public safety initiative. The objection is that banning hoodies or baggy pants is inherently discriminatory, since they are part of a lifestyle that emerged out of a specific type of black culture, which continues to be dominated by black youths. It doesn't take [civil rights activist] Al Sharpton to smell the racism in the air here, especially given the zoot suit precedent of the 1940s. The large boxy

Some argue that banning sagging pants is discriminatory because it is a style dominated by black youth. © Joe Raedle/Getty Images News/Getty Images.

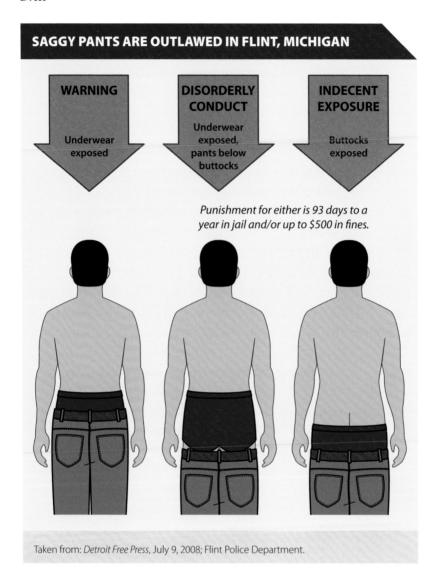

SAGGY PANTS ARE OUTLAWED IN FLINT, MICHIGAN

WARNING

Underwear exposed

DISORDERLY CONDUCT

Underwear exposed, pants below buttocks

INDECENT EXPOSURE

Buttocks exposed

Punishment for either is 93 days to a year in jail and/or up to $500 in fines.

Taken from: *Detroit Free Press*, July 9, 2008; Flint Police Department.

suits, popular among New York blacks and Los Angeles Latinos in the '30s and '40s, were banned by the federal War Production Board on the grounds that they were "extravagant of fabric." The ban was followed by the Zoot Suit Riots of 1943, when sailors on leave in Los Angeles started beating up any Mexicans they could find wearing the outlawed suits.

his shirts do not fall into any of these categories. Palmer's proposed categorical rule, however, is flawed, because it fails to include another type of student speech restriction that schools can institute: content-neutral regulations.

In *Canady*, the plaintiff presented this court with the same categorical argument that Palmer makes, in a facial challenge to a school uniform code. The plaintiff argued that uniforms violated the First Amendment because they banned student clothing that was not disruptive, lewd, or school-sponsored. Judge [Robert] Parker, writing for the court, recognized that the Supreme Court had established these categories for situations in which schools were targeting specific speech but that content-neutral regulations "do not readily conform to [any] of the three categories addressed by the Supreme Court." These cases all addressed "disciplinary action by school officials directed at the political content of student expression," not content-neutral regulations such as school uniforms. . . .

We must decide whether the District's dress code is content-neutral. The District does not allow messages on shirts, but it exempts small logos on shirts and "campus principal approved" shirts that promote school clubs, organizations, athletic teams, or "school spirit." Palmer argues that the dress code's exemption for small logos and school-sponsored shirts by definition violates content-neutrality, because it distinguishes based on content. Similar allegedly-content-based dress code exceptions have been examined by three other federal courts and found to be content-neutral.

Palmer's argument regarding content-neutrality has some judicial support. "As a general rule, laws that by their terms distinguish favored speech from disfavored speech on the basis of the ideas or views expressed are content based," *Turner Broad. Sys., Inc. v. F.C.C.* (1994). A dress code "is content based if it differentiates based on the content of the speech on its face."

The District's code, however, is content-neutral. In its preeminent case on content-neutral regulation, *Ward v. Rock Against*

Some schools ban messages on clothing but not on accessories like backpacks. © Brian Gordon Green/National Geographic/Getty Images.

Racism (1989), the Court stated that "[t]he principal inquiry in determining content-neutrality, in speech cases generally and in time, place, or manner cases in particular, is whether the government has adopted a regulation of speech because of disagreement with the message it conveys." The Court has reiterated this principle. "[A] regulation is generally 'content-neutral' if its restrictions on speech are not based on disagreement with the message it conveys," *Brazos Valley Coal. for Life, Inc. v. City of Bryan, Tex.* (5th Cir. 2005).

The District was in no way attempting to suppress any student's expression through its dress code—a critical fact based on earlier student speech cases—so the dress code is content-neutral. Its allowance for school logos and school-sponsored shirts does not suppress unpopular viewpoints but provides students with more clothing options than they would have had under a complete ban on messages. We therefore employ intermediate scrutiny.

Passing Constitutional Scrutiny

Under intermediate scrutiny, "the School Board's uniform policy will pass constitutional scrutiny (1) if it furthers an important or substantial government interest; (2) if the interest is unrelated to the suppression of student expression; and (3) if the incidental restrictions on First Amendment activities are no more than is necessary to facilitate that interest," *Canady*. Palmer does not contend that the dress code violates the second prong but argues only on the first and third prongs.

Palmer asserts that the code does not further an important or substantial governmental interest. The code's preamble states that the code was adopted "to maintain an orderly and safe learning environment, increase the focus on instruction, promote safety and life-long learning, and encourage professional and responsible dress for all students." The District notes that the code would reduce administrative time spent enforcing the code and promote the school and its activities.

"Improving the educational process is undoubtedly an important interest," *Canady*. Improving student test scores and reducing disciplinary infractions qualify as important governmental interests. Improving student performance, instilling self-confidence, increasing attendance, decreasing disciplinary referrals, and lowering the drop-out rate are all important governmental interests that meet the first prong's requirement. Importantly, this list of recognized interests is not exhaustive, and federal courts should give substantial deference to schools where they present their reasons for passing a given dress code. . . .

The District has provided more than enough evidence to establish its important governmental interests. In *Canady* and *Littlefield*, this court properly set a low bar for the evidence a district must submit to show its dress code meets its stated goals. A statistical showing that the code has improved test scores or lowered disciplinary actions is sufficient. Additionally, evidence of improvements in other districts that have adopted the same or a similar dress code can support the district's decision. . . .

Palmer does not take issue with the school board's claimed interests but instead argues that these interests do not apply, because the board's ban on shirts is undermined by allowing students to wear pins, buttons, wrist-bands, and bumper stickers containing messages. Generally, Palmer believes that allowing messages on buttons destroys the benefit of the dress code and its banning of messages on shirts. For Palmer's objection to stand, however, he would have to show that the District's button allowance destroys all of the District's stated important governmental interests; if any of those stated benefits remain, then the dress code—button/shirt distinction and all—is valid.

The District's stated benefits function under this distinction. Because shirts are large and quite visible, banning them while allowing buttons would still cause less distraction and promote an orderly learning environment. Buttons and pins are also less prominent than are shirts and therefore require less attention from and regulation by teachers. Another District goal—

Setting the Standard for Content-Neutral Regulations

As the courts seek to resolve the jurisprudential confusion surrounding whether *Tinker* or *O'Brien* should be applied to content-neutral regulations in the school setting, they should consider two normative questions that resonate throughout the First Amendment doctrine. First, what level of scrutiny ought to be applied to regulations that incidentally affect student speech? The case law describes *Tinker* as applying a "heightened" standard because of the rigorous nature of the test by which a school district must establish a "substantial disruption" to justify restrictions on student expression. Alternatively, the *O'Brien* test is defined as an "intermediate" level of scrutiny, balancing the interest of the school in regulating speech with the students' rights to free expression. The second normative question that the courts should consider with respect to content-neutral regulations is which standard situates the courts in their proper role, given the deference owed to school authorities in overseeing student conduct.

Geoffrey A. Starks, "Tinker's Tenure in the
School Setting: The Case for Applying O'Brien
to Content-Neutral Regulations," Yale Law
Journal, August 30, 2010.

promoting professional and responsible dress—still functions as well, because students are prepared for a working world in which pins and buttons may be appropriate at work but large, stark political message t-shirts usually are not.

Most importantly, even if, arguendo, we were to find the distinction between messages on shirts and messages on buttons odd, we recognize that the teachers and administrators who establish these rules know better than do we how the distinction will function in schools. "[F]ederal courts should defer to school boards to decide what constitutes appropriate behavior and dress in public school," *Littlefield.* The determination of where to draw lines on dress code decisions "properly rests with the school board, rather than with the federal courts," *Hazelwood.*

Finally, we reject Palmer's "somewhat ironic" argument that the dress code "is an unconstitutional abridgment of speech because it does not abridge enough speech," *Metromedia, Inc. v. City of San Diego* (1981). Under the current dress code, Palmer can come to school with a "John Edwards for President" button or First Amendment wrist-band and express his views through these devices. But Palmer requests that we strike down the dress code because the District gave him this avenue to express himself. He argues that, to survive intermediate scrutiny, the code must allow him no options at all.

We decline to follow this perverse reasoning. Under Palmer's rule, school districts would rush to impose the strictest dress codes possible or merely require school uniforms. Students such as Palmer would never be able to express their views through any medium. We eschew any legal principle that would lead to such a race-to-the-bottom.

> "T-shirts may intrude upon our lives in
> the public sphere, but they're also our
> most vivid reminder that free speech is
> woven into the fabric of our culture."

Free Expression on Clothing Is an Important Right for High School Students

Greg Beato

In the following viewpoint, Greg Beato proclaims that T-shirts and other clothing with controversial messages are a vital part of free expression and raise public awareness without intrusion. In the aftermath of the 1999 Columbine High School shooting and the September 11, 2001, terrorist attacks, he explains, schools have cracked down on such messages through dress codes and uniform policies. However, the author insists that students who wear such clothing demonstrate an active engagement in civic life and attract attention to social and political issues. Beato is a writer whose articles have appeared in many publications, including the San Francisco Chronicle, Spin, Reason, *and* Wired.

On April 29 [2008] a grassroots army of teenaged billboards, provocatively packaged in combed cotton agitprop, will be

Greg Beato, "I'm With Stupid: The Perennially Embattled Free Speech Zone Over Our Chests," *Reason*, April 2008, pp. 20–21. Copyright © 2008 by Reason Foundation. All rights reserved. Reproduced by permission.

deployed across the land. Their goal? Raise consciousness, spark discussion, and, if all goes according to plan, get thrown out of class. The occasion is the sixth annual National Pro-Life T-Shirt Day.

"When school administrators harass students, tell them they can't wear the shirt, it raises awareness," says Erik Whittington, director of Rock for Life, the group that organizes the event. "The media gets a hold of it. The word gets out. The more people who hear the phrase on the shirt, the more we educate people."

This year, Whittington says his organization has big plans. To promote Pro-Life T-Shirt Day, they're creating a Rock for Life website where the young pronatalist participants can network with each other. It'll be like MySpace or Facebook, except that instead of connecting over a common interest in drunken snapshots and copyright infringement, the teens will bond via a shared passion for fetuses. Even with such Web 2.0 accessorizing, however, the key to the event's potency remains the all-powerful T-shirt. "It has abortion in big letters," says Whittington of this year's model. "Then we have three graphics side by side. The first two are images of small children in the womb at early stages. The third image is blank. Under those images, it reads, "Growing. Growing. Gone.""

T-Shirts Get in Your Face

Considering all the incendiary polemics that characterize both sides of the abortion divide, this rhetorical dinger is fairly benign. Yet some kind of escalatory alchemy occurs when free speech is wedded to casual wear; the mildly provocative becomes untenable, the sophomoric too obscene to bear. Compared to sexier media devices like, say, the iPhone, T-shirts are pretty clunky. Their storage capacity is limited. They're not Bluetooth-enabled. And yet they boast a sense of intimacy and authority few other content delivery systems can match. They come, after all, with a living, breathing byline attached. They're far more mobile than other forms of meat-space spam, such as billboards and posters; they literally get in your face.

It can be argued that message T-shirts convey a student's active participation in social and political causes and are thus an important form of free expression. © Emmanuel Dunand/ AFP/Getty Images.

In January of this year, several visitors wearing T-shirts emblazoned with various impeach [former President George W.] Bush and [former Vice President Dick] Cheney messages claimed that security guards at the National Archives Building— the place where the original version of the First Amendment now resides—barred them from the premises. In 1991, in the wake of the Gulf War, the Kuwaiti government sentenced one man to 15 years in jail simply for wearing a Saddam Hussein T-shirt. Today in the United States, we're far more enlightened: Selling a T-shirt inscribed with the names of military personnel who died in Iraq will only get you a maximum sentence of one year in Louisiana and Oklahoma.

Are you against sodomy or breast cancer? In favor of "hot moms" or [politician] John Edwards? In 2007 each of these convictions got at least one high school student kicked out of class. In Wisconsin, Edgerton High School enforces a zero tolerance policy against Insane Clown Posse T-shirts. In Aurora, Illinois, all it takes to earn a trip to the principal's office is a T-shirt with a large dollar sign on it.

How did endorsing capitalism or B-list presidential candidates become so controversial? In the 1980s and '90s, hoping to crack down on intracurricular violence and crime, a growing number of schools resorted to the sartorial [clothing] communism of dress codes and uniforms. As President Bill Clinton put it in 1996, "If it means that teenagers will stop killing each other over designer jackets, then our public schools should be able to require their students to wear school uniforms." In the wake of the 1999 Columbine High School massacre, message T-shirts and any other style of dress that undermined the notion that high school students were the new maximum-security inmates fell under suspicion. In the wake of 9/11—Columbine for adults—this attitude spilled over into our malls, airports, and presidential town hall meetings.

It's not just high school massacres and terrorist attacks that have left us so intolerant of our fellow citizens' chests. During the last decade, pretty much every major media innovation—Fox News, Google, Napster, iTunes, Digg—has involved filtering information more precisely, giving us more and more control over the data we ingest. But that uncompromising raw-foods zealot at the organic farmer's market whose shirt reads "Chewing is murder"? Or the perky fetus hugger who wants you to know that "Mean abortionists suck"? [Apple chief executive officer] Steve Jobs hasn't figured out a way to delete them from your life yet.

"If people don't want to listen to you, what makes you think they want to hear from your sweater?" the satirist Fran Lebowitz quipped in her 1978 essay collection *Metropolitan Life*, published when message T-shirts were enjoying their first wave of cultural ubiquity. What this sentiment doesn't acknowledge is that it's exactly because people don't want to listen to us that the drive-by evangelism of T-shirts is so enduring. Body-borne messages can't be muted, fast forwarded, unsubscribed, banished to the "ignore" list, opted out of, or dumped in the recycle bin. Unlike telemarketers or Jehovah's Witnesses, they don't invade anyone's privacy. Their zero-decibel proselytizing is simultaneously low-key and obtrusive. . . .

But They're Good for Us

Instead of avoiding such encounters with the dye-sublimated "Other," we should embrace them as a kind of civic spinach: While we may not enjoy them, they're good for us. In *Tinker v. Des Moines*, the landmark 1969 case in which the U.S. Supreme Court determined that high school students have a First Amendment right to express political and social opinions in school settings, Justice Abe Fortas observed that "any word spoken, in class, in the lunchroom, or on the campus, that deviates from the views of another person may start an argument or cause a disturbance. But our Constitution says that we must take this risk; and our history says that it is this sort of hazardous freedom—this kind of openness—that is the basis of our national strength and of the

Political T-Shirts Are Usually Only Offensive to Some

Schools have banned political t-shirts in the United States because of their offensive nature. Two such cases were those of Bretton Barber, who wore a t-shirt stating that George Bush was an international terrorist, and Timothy Gies, whose shirts regularly displayed various symbols signifying peace or anarchy and an upside-down American flag. If we apply the offence principle to these cases, it would be hard for a school to argue that the t-shirts caused such offence as to warrant their ban. Neither school had a uniform policy. Regarding the questions of extent and duration, the boys wore the t-shirts to school on an inconsistent and irregular basis, and so these matters are hard to gauge. The t-shirts did not cause a major disruption to the education in the school. The t-shirts did not appear to be morally offensive to a *large* number of people. Finally, the intensity of the offence was questionable. Wearing a t-shirt that provides a general political message such as "anarchy" or "peace" does not seem *de facto* [in fact] offensive. Similarly, whilst the t-shirt against George W. Bush may have been morally offensive to some, it is not clear that the intensity of the offence is on the same level as other morally offensive symbols (such as the swastika or the white hooded Ku Klux Klan gown) where the offensiveness is generally agreed across society.

Richard Pring and Mark Halstead, The Common School and the Comprehensive Ideal: A Defence by Richard Pring with Complementary Essays. *Malden, MA: Wiley-Blackwell, 2008.*

independence and vigor of Americans who grow up and live in this relatively permissive, often disputatious society."

In the late 1990s era of no-logo vogue, cultural commentators fretted that the once-democratic medium of the T-shirt had been co-opted by corporations, and that T-shirt buyers were concerned only with raising the planet's Hilfiger consciousness and saving the FUBUs. "The slogans on contemporary T-shirts are increasingly meaningless," the novelist and columnist Russell Smith observed in the *Globe and Mail* in 2000. "Most of them are simply the brand name of the T-shirt itself."

Now that our T-shirts are so blithely outspoken—and deliberately offensive—on every issue from Medicare to [singer] Britney Spears, it sometimes seems as if we'd like to ban our way back to a more sartorially decorous era. Ultimately, however, the T-shirt skirmishes that continuously erupt are oddly reassuring. Can the public schools be as out of control as they're often alleged to be if all it takes to get suspended from one is an "I [heart] My Wiener" shirt? Has our public sphere grown as hopelessly coarse as our loudest cultural scrub maids insist if a shirt featuring a faux fishing theme and the phrase "Master Baiter" is enough to make Southwest Airlines ground you?

Shouldn't we take comfort in the fact that so many high school students are ready to fight for their right to champion the unborn, maternal hotties, and whatever else they can think of to test the limits of *Tinker v. Des Moines*? T-shirts may intrude upon our lives in the public sphere, but they're also our most vivid reminder that free speech is woven into the fabric of our culture.

> *"In recent years, a growing number of teenagers have been dressing to articulate—or confound—gender identity and sexual orientation."*

Cross Dressing Is a Growing Challenge for Schools

Jan Hoffman

In the following viewpoint, Jan Hoffman writes that students are increasingly exploring gender boundaries and sexual orientation through clothing, which challenges educators. Some schools limit or discipline such expressions, she states, and must consider anti-discrimination policies, psychological issues, community values, and campus disruption and safety. Others are more tolerant, allowing students to cross dress within prescribed dress codes, Hoffman explains. Acceptance is inconsistent among students, but their generation is more open than adults to transgender identities, she concludes. The author is a reporter for the New York Times *who covers style and adolescents.*

By now, most high school dress codes have just about done away with the guesswork.

Girls: no midriff-baring blouses, stiletto heels, miniskirts.

Boys: no sagging pants, muscle shirts.

But do the math.

"Rules" + "teenager" = "challenges."

If the skirt is an acceptable length, can a boy wear it?

Can a girl attend her prom in a tuxedo?

In recent years, a growing number of teenagers have been dressing to articulate—or confound—gender identity and sexual orientation. Certainly they have been confounding school officials, whose responses have ranged from indifference to applause to bans.

Last week [in November 2009], a cross-dressing Houston senior was sent home because his wig violated the school's dress code rule that a boy's hair may not be "longer than the bottom of a regular shirt collar." In October, officials at a high school in Cobb County, Ga., sent home a boy who favored wigs, makeup and skinny jeans. In August, a Mississippi student's senior portrait was barred from her yearbook because she had posed in a tuxedo.

Other schools are more accepting of unconventional gender expression. In September, a freshman girl at Rincon High School in Tucson who identifies as male was nominated for homecoming prince. Last May, a gay male student at a Los Angeles high school was crowned prom queen.

Dress code conflicts often reflect a generational divide, with students coming of age in a culture that is more accepting of ambiguity and difference than that of the adults who make the rules.

"This generation is really challenging the gender norms we grew up with," said Diane Ehrensaft, an Oakland psychologist who writes about gender. "A lot of youths say they won't be bound by boys having to wear this or girls wearing that. For them, gender is a creative playing field." Adults, she added, "become the gender police through dress codes."

Dress is always code, particularly for teenagers eager to telegraph evolving identities. Each year, schools hope to quell disruption by prohibiting the latest styles that signify a gang affiliation, a sexual act or drug use.

Ceara Sturgis (left) with her mother, Veronica Rodriguez. In Sturgis's school yearbook photo she was not allowed to wear a tuxedo as the male students are required to. © AP Images/ Rogelio V. Solis.

But when officials want to discipline a student whose wardrobe expresses sexual orientation or gender variance, they must consider anti-discrimination policies, mental health factors, community standards and classroom distractions.

And safety is a critical concern. In February 2008, Lawrence King, an eighth-grader from Oxnard, Calif., who occasionally wore high-heeled boots and makeup, was shot to death in class by another student.

Gender-Boundary Questions Are on the Rise

Although dress code disputes are largely anecdotal, popping up in the news when a lawsuit threat emerges, educators and psychologists say that more schools will have to address them in the near future. There are 4,118 gay-straight alliance clubs in high schools across the country, which raise awareness of such issues. Gender-boundary questions are even bubbling up in elementary schools, with parents seeking to pave the way for their children, in blogs like acceptingdad.com and labelsareforjars.wordpress.com.

At minimum, more students are trying on their curiosity for size. Typically during "Mix 'n' Match Day," at Ramapo High School in Spring Valley, N.Y., students might wear polka dots with stripes, said Diane Schneider, a teacher who is a chairwoman of the Hudson Valley chapter of the Gay, Lesbian and Straight Education Network. But this year, she said, "about 50 kids came as cross-dressers."

All this is too much for some educators, who say high school should not be a public stage to work out private identity issues. School, they say, is a rigorous academic and social training ground for the world of adults and employment.

"It's hard enough to get kids to concentrate on an algorithm—even without Jimmy sitting there in lipstick and fake eyelashes," said Kay Hymowitz, a senior fellow at the Manhattan Institute.

Because schools are communal, she wrote in an e-mail message, "self-expression will always have to be at least partially limited, just as it is in the workplace." Principals need leeway in determining how students present themselves, she added. "You can understand why a lot of principals get fed up with these sorts of fights and just decide on school uniforms."

At Wesson Attendance Center, a Mississippi public school, just that sort of fight erupted over senior portraits. Last summer, during her photo session, Ceara Sturgis, 17, dutifully tried on the traditional black drape, the open-necked robe that reveals the collarbone, a hint of bare shoulder.

"It was terrible!" said Ms. Sturgis, an honors student, band president and soccer goalie, who has been openly gay since 10th grade. "If you put a boy in a drape, that's me! I have big shoulders and ooh, it didn't look like me! I said, 'I can't do this!' So my mom said, 'Try on the tux.' And that looked normal."

Shortly thereafter, students were informed that girls had to wear drapes for yearbook portraits; boys, tuxedos.

The Mississippi chapter of the American Civil Liberties Union wrote to the school. Rickey Clopton, superintendent of Copiah County schools, did not return phone calls. Last month he released a statement affirming that the school's decision was "based upon sound educational policy and legal precedent."

Last month, Veronica Rodriguez, Ms. Sturgis's mother, paid for a full-page ad in the yearbook that is to include a photograph of her daughter in a tuxedo.

Dress code challenges like these have been cropping up for years. Earlier this year, when prodded by lawyers, schools in Jackson, Miss., and Lebanon, Ind., reversed policies and allowed girls to wear tuxedos.

But generally, courts give local administrators great latitude. In Marion County, Fla., students must dress "in keeping with their gender." Last spring, when a boy came to school wearing high-heeled boots, a stuffed bra, and a V-neck T-shirt, he was sent home to change.

"He was cross-dressing, and it caused a disruption in the normal instructional day," said Kevin Christian, a district spokesman. "That's the whole point behind the dress code."

The Line Between Classroom Distraction and Self-Expression

In some districts, administrators seek to define the line between classroom distraction and the student's need for self-expression. A few years ago, when Dr. Alan Storm was assistant superintendent at Sunnyside Unified School District in Tucson, he oversaw legal and disciplinary matters.

Principals would ask him about dress code gender cases: "They'd say, 'Johnny just showed up in a cutoff top! Should I suspend the kid or make him change his clothes?'" Dr. Storm recalled. "And I'd say, 'Is there a bare midriff?' 'No.' 'Then it doesn't violate your dress code. You have no right to make the kid change his clothes. But it's your absolute policy to keep the kid safe.'"

Dr. Storm, now superintendent of a technological program for high school students throughout Pima County, Ariz., helped draft anti-discrimination policies that protect gender expression and sexual orientation, since adopted by some Tucson districts.

Such policies have become woven into the social fabric of Rincon High School, said Brenda Kazen, a school counselor. "Gender expression is very fluid here." Some boys have worn makeup and pink frilly scarves; girls wear big T-shirts, long basketball shorts—and look like male gang members, she said. Moreover, the student population includes immigrants from more than three dozen countries. "Our kids are just used to seeing different things, and they're O.K. with it," Ms. Kazen said.

Acceptance Is Hardly Unilateral
Yet acceptance is hardly unilateral among teenagers, much less adults.

"There are other places where there are real safety issues," said Barbara Risman, a sociologist at the University of Illinois who studies adolescent gender identity. "Most boys still very much feel the need to repress whole parts of themselves to avoid peer harassment."

Last fall, Stephen Russell, a professor at the University of Arizona who studies gay, lesbian and transgender youths, conducted a survey of about 1,200 California high school students. When asked why those perceived as not as "masculine" or "feminine" as others were harassed, a leading reason students gave was "manner of dress."

Often a student's clothes, intended as a fashion statement, can be misread as a billboard about sexuality. In recent years, "emo" style has moved from punk fringe almost to pop mainstream, with boys wearing heavy eyeliner, body-hugging T-shirts and floppy hair dyed black, to emulate singers like Adam Lambert and Pete Wentz.

"The emo kids get a lot of grief," said Marty Hulsey, a guidance counselor at a school near Auburn, Ala. "Even teachers say things and I had to stop it. One child came to me who was an emo kid and said he was accused of being gay but that he had a girlfriend." Mr. Hulsey said he affirmed the boy's right to wear the clothes that expressed his taste.

When a principal asks a boy to leave his handbag at home, is the request an attempt to protect a student from harassment or harassment itself?

Dress codes should be enforced consistently, with measures also taken against straight students who dress provocatively, said Diane Levin, a professor at Wheelock College in Boston who writes about the sexualization of young children.

But whether a principal bans gender-blurring clothing, she said, the student cannot be abandoned. Why has the student chosen to dress this way? "Is the student sensation-seeking?" Dr. Levin asked. "Can the school keep the student safe?"

Changing Student Perceptions

Some guidance counselors say that while safety concerns cannot be dismissed, high school administrators shouldn't presume that such students will be targeted by peers.

Jeff Grace, faculty adviser for a gay-straight alliance club at high school in Columbus, Ohio, said he has seen student perceptions change over the last decade.

One student, Mr. Grace recounted, born male and named Jack, has long, straight hair and prefers to be referred to with a female pronoun. Jack is careful not to violate the dress code. She favors tops that are tapered but not revealing, flats, [and] lip gloss.

"One day I heard a student say, 'Man, there was a girl in the guy's restroom, standing up using the urinal! What's up with that?'" Mr. Grace recalled.

Bathrooms can be dangerous for transgender students. But the other student replied off-handedly, "That wasn't a girl. That's just Jack."

Organizations to Contact

The editors have compiled the following list of organizations concerned with the issues debated in this book. The descriptions are derived from materials provided by the organizations. All have publications or information available for interested readers. The list was compiled on the date of publication of the present volume; the information provided here may change. Be aware that many organizations take several weeks or longer to respond to queries, so allow as much time as possible.

American-Arab Anti-Discrimination Committee (ADC)

1732 Wisconsin Ave. NW, Washington, DC 20007
(202) 244-2990 • fax: (202) 333-3980
website: www.adc.org
e-mail: adc@adc.org

ADC is a civil rights organization committed to defending the rights of people of Arab descent and promoting their rich cultural heritage. ADC, which is nonprofit, nonsectarian and nonpartisan, is the largest Arab-American grassroots civil rights organization in the United States. Founded in 1980, it has chapters nationwide; is headquartered in Washington, DC; and operates offices in Massachusetts, Michigan, and New Jersey. ADC welcomes members of all faiths, backgrounds, and ethnicities.

American Civil Liberties Union (ACLU)

125 Broad Street, 18th Floor, New York, NY 10004
website: www.aclu.org

The ACLU champions the rights set forth in the Declaration of Independence and the Constitution, and it opposes censoring any form of speech. The ACLU publishes several handbooks, public policy reports, project reports, civil liberties books, and pamphlets. It also offers "StandUp!" a web page for students.

Center for Public Education
1680 Duke Street, Alexandria, VA 22314
(703) 838-6722 • fax: (703) 548-5613
website: www.centerforpubliceducation.org
e-mail: centerforpubliced@nsba.org

The Center for Public Education is a resource center set up by the National School Boards Association (NSBA). The Center for Public Education works to provide information about public education, leading to more understanding about our schools, more community-wide involvement, and better decision-making by school leaders on behalf of all students in their classrooms. Among the many publications available at the center's website is *Free Speech and Public Schools.*

First Amendment Center
555 Pennsylvania Ave., Washington, DC 20001
(202) 292-6288 • fax: (202) 292-6295
website: www.firstamendmentcenter.org
e-mail: info@fac.org

The center serves as a forum for the study and exploration of free-expression issues, including freedom of speech, of the press and of religion, and the rights to assemble and to petition the government. The center's programs provide education and information to the public and groups including First Amendment scholars and experts, educators, government policy makers, legal experts, and students. The center is nonpartisan and does not lobby or litigate.

Islamic Society of North America (ISNA)
PO Box 38, Plainfield, IN 46168
(317) 839-8157 • fax: (317) 839-1840
website: www.isna.net

ISNA is an association of Muslim organizations and individuals that provides a common platform for presenting Islam; supporting Muslim communities; developing educational, social and outreach programs; and fostering good relations with other religious communities, and civic and service organizations. It operates a Youth Programming and Services Department and Muslim Youth North America (MYNA).

National Coalition Against Censorship (NCAC)

275 Seventh Ave., Suite 1504, New York, NY 10001
(212) 807-6222 • fax: (212) 807-6245
website: www.ncac.org
e-mail: ncac@ncac.org

NCAC is an alliance of fifty-two participating organizations dedicated to protecting free expression and access to information. It has many projects dedicated to educating the public and protecting free expression, including the Free Expression Policy Project, the Kids' Right to Read Project, The Knowledge Project: Censorship and Science, and the Youth Free Expression Network. Among its publications is *The First Amendment in Schools*.

National School Safety Center (NSSC)

141 Duesenberg Drive, Suite 7B, Westlake Village, CA 91362
(805) 373-9977
website: www.schoolsafety.us
e-mail: info@schoolsafety.us

NSSC serves as an advocate for safe, secure, and peaceful schools worldwide and as a catalyst for the prevention of school crime and violence. It provides school communities and their school safety partners with information, resources, consultation, and training services. The center offers books, videos, and resource papers.

National Youth Rights Association (NYRA)

1101 15th Street NW, Suite 200
Washington, DC, 20005
(202) 835-1739
website: www.youthrights.org

NYRA is a youth-led national nonprofit organization dedicated to fighting for the civil rights and liberties of young people. NYRA has more than seven thousand members representing all fifty states. It seeks to lower the voting age, lower the drinking age, repeal curfew laws, and protect student rights.

For Further Reading

Books

David L. Brunsma, *The School Uniform Movement and What It Tells Us About American Education: A Symbolic Crusade.* Lanham, MD: Scarecrow Education, 2004.

David L. Brunsma, *Uniforms in Public Schools: A Decade of Research and Debate.* Lanham, MD: Rowman & Littlefield Education, 2006.

Kenneth Dautrich and David A. Yalof, *The Future of the First Amendment: The Digital Media, Civic Education, and Free Expression Rights in America's High Schools.* Lanham, MD: Rowman & Littlefield Education, 2008.

Anne Proffitt Dupree, *Speaking Up: The Unintended Costs of Free Speech in Public Schools.* Cambridge, MA: Harvard University Press, 2009.

Dianne Gereluk, *Symbolic Clothing in Schools: What Should Be Worn and Why.* New York: Continuum, 2008.

Susan Dudley Gold, *Tinker v. Des Moines: Free Speech for Students.* Tarrytown, NY: Marshall Cavendish Benchmark, 2007.

Thomas A. Jacobs, *Teens Take It to Court: Young People Who Challenged the Law—and Changed Your Life.* Minneapolis, MN: Free Spirit, 2006.

Anthony Lewis, *Freedom for the Thought That We Hate: A Biography of the First Amendment.* New York: Basic Books, 2008.

Emma Tarlo, *Visibly Muslim: Fashion, Politics, Faith.* New York: Berg, 2010.

Periodicals and Internet Sources

Peter Applebome, "In Court: When Clothes Speak to More Than Fashion," *New York Times*, September 23, 2007.

John Bell, "Dress Code," *Today's OEA* [Oregon Education Association], February 2010.

Jessica Bennett, "Fashion Police: Flint Cracks Down on Sagging," *Daily Beast*, July 17, 2008.

Marsha Boutelle, "Uniforms: Are They a Good Fit?," *Education Digest*, February 2008.

Matt Buesing, "Dress Code Adoption: A Year's Worth of Steps," *School Administrator*, April 2011.

Theodore Dalrymple, "Wrong From Head to Toe," *National Review*, March 28, 2005.

Ian Evans, "The Dress Code: Some Black College Students Embrace the Business-Casual Dress Code with Personal Style," *Black Collegian*, September 2008.

Alex Johnson, "Students, Parents Bare Claws over Dress Codes," msnbc.com, October 18, 2008.

Amanda Knief, "Liberté, Egalité—de Féministes! Revealing the Burqa as a Pro-Choice Issue," *The Humanist*, September/October 2010.

Tanya Marcum and Sandra J. Perry, "Dressed for Success: Can a Claim of Religious Discrimination Be Successful?," *Labor Law Journal*, Winter 2010.

Shauna Pomerantz, "Cleavage in a Tank Top: Bodily Prohibition and the Discourses of School Dress Codes," *Alberta Journal of Education Research*, Winter 2007.

Time, "Fighting for Free Speech in Schools," May 10, 2007.

Bob Unruh, "Cross-Dressing Day Sparks School Exodus," *World Net Daily*, November 28, 2007.

Danielle Urban, "Should Your School's Dress Code Address Transgender Students?," *Education Update*, January 2010.

Bill Ward, "Muslim Athletes Keeping the Faith," *Tampa Tribune*, March 30, 2008.

Index